FREE AIR-CONDITIONING

WITH A POPCORN SCENT!

Roxanne Lord

Disclaimer: These stories are told from my viewpoint and to the best of my memory.

{To Marty}

Copyright 2023 Roxanne Lord
All rights reserved. No part of this book may be reproduced or used in any manner without the prior written permission of the copyright owner, except for the use of brief quotations in a book review.

To request permission, contact the publisher at
publishing@theavanttech.com.

Hardcover: 979-8-9869016-4-0
Ebook: 979-8-9869016-5-7

Proofread by Gail Binkly

Published by Emi Cornelius – Avant Tech Consulting
www.theavanttech.com
publishing@theavanttech.com

Introduction

The first time I ever tried sales it was as a seven-year-old Bluebird (young Campfire Girls) when I was sent out to sell Almond Roca as a fundraiser. The first door I knocked on was answered by an elder lady. She said no, she didn't need any Almond Roca, and I was so devastated the tears started tracking down my cheeks. She felt so sorry for me (and who wouldn't? It was epic! Sob-hitching voice and everything when I apologized for disturbing her) that she decided her grandkids would enjoy it and bought everything I had. And though some might see that result as proving natural talent, I was convinced otherwise, and I managed to avoid selling anything for many years after. So, I still have no real clue how it is that 20 years later I became a sole proprietor of a Main Street shop because it rather defies understanding but, I did. For twenty-three years I rented a small shop (336 square feet, including the 48 square feet of storage) from the local theatre; all of those years on a handshake deal. First it was Punchak's Paperbacks, a used book shop that I opened in 1995, and then it was Kokopelli's Getaways, a tourist shop with all-original inventory that I converted the bookstore into in 2012. I came to view my shop as my version of the world wide web, a place that brought interesting neighbors, customers and other random people into my life for short interactions and conversations. And so this book is structured; not as chapter and verse (since it has neither chapters nor verses) but as short interactions, conversations, and reflections. It was always fun to see who the wind might blow my way on any given day as I do tend to attract real characters. Which means, of course, if you are reading this...

29 West Main Street

I found it a challenge, choosing names for my shops. When I was a bookstore, Lord's Books was definitely out (unless I wanted people to think I was a Christian bookstore and I was a soul proprietor rather than a sole proprietor) but thankfully, I did like the rhyming alliteration of Punchak's Paperbacks (Punchak is my husband Marty's last name) and so I went with that. I added a "Get Lit!" motto and I was on my way. Kokopelli's Getaways, however, was not as easily resolved. The idea for the shop was to do something that featured our dog but that would also make sense to why tourists come here: The Four Corners, USA. The Four Corners area is called the archaeological capital of the United States because of Mesa Verde and thousands of other archaeological sites. There is plenty of rock art (pictographs and petroglyphs) dating from the Anasazi/Ancient Puebloan period (Anasazi was the original common term, and then it became Ancient Puebloans) and Kokopelli is one of the most common figures depicted. And, he is very popular with tourists, so we decided to incorporate him. (What can I say? Yes, we shamelessly used a favored character to accompany our dog to draw folks in.) Marty wasn't directly involved with my shops; nevertheless, I did manage to convince him to do the drawings for my inventory, despite his claims that he's an engineer, not an artist. He couldn't deny me after I pointed out that what I was looking for were vignettes similar to the ones he drew for me when we were a young couple, dating from a distance because he was in the Army and stationed overseas, showing what we'd do together when he got home. Thus, the concept for the tourist shop became depictions of our notion of what Kokopelli would be doing in our area if he was around today, which would, of course, involve a fur-friend. We then titled the depictions with "Get" idioms, starting with "Get Lit" to honor the bookstore and so, Kokopelli's "Getaways" seemed a good fit. Who did I know would absolutely leave with a purchase? Those who asked for the dog's name: Happy, the Queen of Happy-ness, who wondered why Kokopelli got top billing and it wasn't "Happy's Getaways". We did make some headway with the age-before-beauty argument but are not convinced she ever fully accepted it, even though I referred to my shop as the Happy-est place on earth, where you could take Happy memories and leave a smile behind.

Though I did come to view my shop as my version of the world wide web, the fact remains that I couldn't offer free Wi-Fi as a lure for folks to come into my shop for many of those years because, ahem, there wasn't yet widespread wireless internet. However, it turns out that I found something else enticing. It used to be I'd say 100s are for test scores and not temperatures but then I learned that those degrees can also be good for business. My shop was on the theatre's duct system and the theatre cranking the a/c for the movie-goers meant it was so cold in my shop in the summer that even though I closed the vent as far as I could without it whistling, I still wore a sweater or ran a space heater by my desk. Then one day, I had a sweaty guy come into my shop to buy a t-shirt to change into and he rhapsodized so vocally on how nice it was to be in such a cool space I thought, "I should make up a 'Free air-conditioning' sign for my door." And so I did, and almost immediately had people coming in to cool off. Then the mail carrier came in and remarked that the sign would give people something new to comment on; something other than the smell of popcorn in my shop. (It was inevitable, being on the theatre's ducts, that the smell of popcorn would waft on in. And apparently also inevitable that folks would point it out to me–like I somehow didn't know–because I surely never noticed. "Do you smell that? It smells like popcorn in here!") And so I thought, "Even better! A sign that says "Free air-conditioning... with a popcorn scent!" And it did indeed become an even greater talking point, from folks trying to figure out where the scent was coming from (you'd be surprised how many never guessed the vent, and how accomplished folks who did guess it felt) to the gentleman who came in and said, "Saw it, read it–came in and–felt it, smelt it." My favorite has to have been when a tourist came in with his dog, Milo. (Well-behaved dogs were welcome in my shop.) The dog came over and laid down by me at my desk (the air-conditioner was right above me) and lopped his tail a few times like he was saying, "No hurry, take your time, I'm good right here." When it was time to go, the pupper didn't want to leave, so the man laid his hand on the dog's head in a Vulcan mind-meld gesture and asked him, "What's the problem?" then waited a beat before turning to me and saying, "Milo didn't want us to leave without me thanking you for the free popcorn-scented air-conditioning." And Milo then wagged his tail goodbye and they left. That sign was so popular that it went up every year by the first official day of tourist season. (Probably on the first unofficial one too but, I couldn't find an Unofficial to ask what day that was.)

I saw on the news one morning that you could be fired for criticizing your boss on social media sites and thought, "Oooohhhh, now there's a multiple personality disorder just waiting to happen for a sole proprietor with no employees." So, when I went online that night, I complained about how, "That witch I work for just sits around reading, singing, seat-dancing. That's because I'm the one doing all the work. I mean geez, I had to go next door to the theatre to get her some chocolate-covered almonds because she insisted, all the while muttering about thunder and lightning and rain, like candy is the magic elixir that will stop her from melting or something. She's such a pill but sadly, not an antidote." The theatre manager at the time liked that so much that on the next rainy day, they brought the almonds over to me, and thus began a running commentary about my relationship with that witch (*cough* me *cough*) I worked for, and all the ways she made my life miserable. As you'll see, as you read on.

Back in 1995, when I was looking for retail space, I checked out a number of rentals before I landed where I was. (In a nice bit of small-town serendipity, my folks were telling the barber that I was looking when they got their haircuts and he had a relative getting ready to move out of the space I was to occupy.) One of them was a deal where I thought the people were looking to rent space but no, they wanted to partner with a "respectable business front" for the business they proposed to open: a sex toy shop. They thought a bookshop a great idea, as, "We'd both be opening people's minds." Me, "I'm not Elmo (a Tacoma WA reference, where I was raised, to adult bookstores) and from my point of view, that'd be sending my business a bit south of the mind." Yeah, that was a no but my Mom sure got a kick out of making up store names. I think "Books and Nooks" had to be my favorite.

Shortly after I opened Punchak's Paperbacks I had a bunch of paraphernalia made up with my shop logo and "Get Lit!" motto. (That would be t-shirts and hats and mugs, for those who just incorrectly assumed "paraphernalia" was referring to weed-related items. Yep, busted.) Marty's brother John, an ironworker (now retired) in the DC area (one of those guys you see walking around on girders 30 stories high. Their union motto is, "We do our own stunts") was continuously in one of the t-shirts when Marty was visiting, so Marty remarked that he was glad he was enjoying them so much. That's when he learned that his brother went out of his way to wear the t-shirts because he was wearing it one day and some "important DC person" who seemed to think the world should stop when he walked by, thought it appropriate to remark on how ignorant ironworkers are, so ignorant they go around advertising their low-class behavior on their clothing. John didn't so much appreciate the attitude or the remark so he said to the man, "Lit means literature... dumbass." He so enjoyed the slack-jawed response to that, and all the similar interactions that followed, he practically lived in those t-shirts. Then we heard tell about our nephew being challenged by his school administration over his shirt. His only recourse was to do the implied, "Lit means literature..." by showing them the back of it, which clearly showed my "Punchak's Paperbacks" logo. But apparently, Lit isn't Lit except when it is (English Lit, French Lit, etc.) and his supposedly wasn't, so they sent him home to change it, anyway. (Because yes, dumbasses.) And then a friend who wore his t-shirt while answering his jury summons was peremptorily dismissed, without even having been asked a question; though sadly, also without ever getting to say, "Lit means literature... dumbass." Who knew the t-shirts from the bookstore would be a statement piece? Such a good one that I was more than happy to adopt "Lit means literature... dumbass" as my unofficial slogan.

Before I opened a shop, I'd have thought that it would occur to people that when they cup their hands around their face and lean in to look into the window of a clearly open business that they might just find themselves looking directly into someone's face but no, it really didn't, even when they had to look around the "open" sign to see in. Little kids were the best. They would accept that they were being nosy when they'd stick their nose up against the glass on your door to see inside and just smile and wave back when I'd wave at them. (I put a tote hanging at their height on the door, so they'd have something to look at besides just me, and they got such a kick out of that.) Adults, on the other hand, would pop back like a jack-in-the box when they realized they were looking right at me. Now, retail being what it is, I had busy days, and I had slow days. And during slow times I would tend to crank the tunes and sing, maybe dance around a little. Many adults who caught me at it tended to get a kind of embarrassed smile and back up. I'd just grin at them. But not so with kids. They'd see me singing and seat-dancing through the bottom of the window and they'd start dancing right along with me. I would get such a kick out of them while thinking to myself that ten years later, they'd be the young primpers, on their way to a movie date, checking out their style and moves in my window. I was often tempted to make up Olympic-style rating cards to put up. "9.5 for presentation/8 for technical skill." The gold medal would surely have gone to the young man using the glass as a mirror to do a muscle flex test before taking a little shot of breath spray.

I had a man who came into the bookstore about once a year to share pictures of his vacation trips. He was not a story teller by nature so I asked lots of questions to hear about his experiences. On one such occasion I asked him his favorite thing and he said, "The monkeys." Naturally, I started looking for monkeys in his photos but photography was also not a strength of his so our conversation went, "Is that a monkey?" "No." "Well, that's gotta be a monkey, there." "Nope." We did that particular back-and-forth a number of times, with me paying particular attention to the trees and any blobs I saw in them until he finally said, in a reached-his-limit-with-my-idiocy tone, "Let me be perfectly clear. THERE ARE NO MONKEYS IN THESE PICTURES!" (What was I thinking?! My bad!)

Who knew I had such a talent for making folks feel young again?! I had a gentleman in the shop who had, among other things, been telling me how ancient he was. He stayed long enough for me to consider it polite to request his name and he said, "James Buchanan. You remember the president?" Me, "No, a little before my time, but I'm happy to meet you, now. So, what've you been up to all these years?" It took him a second and then, "Hey, I'm not THAT ancient!!" And, I have to say, there was a new spring in his step when he left.

Life in the bookstore lane: Though I owned a bookstore for sixteen years, I rarely discussed books, in depth, with the people who came in. I tried book clubs a few times but they were so unlike the vigorous debates I was accustomed to in the seminar-based college I attended that I didn't stick with it long. One of the rare exceptions was a man named Denton who opened a hardback bookstore outside of town shortly after I opened my shop. He came in one day to see what I carried and with clear disappointment on his face he said, "This is what you read?" (My shop was overwhelmingly leisure reading... or trash, if you prefer.) I said, "Sure. Sometimes. What do you read?" He told me he used to be a college professor, and preferred more strenuous books. I said, "That's cool. I do the academic thing on occasion, too." And thus began a near-twenty-year relationship of discussion, debate and the exchange of ideas between two people with a forty-year age spread and a wealth of different perspectives to share. Whenever he was in town and had the time, he'd stop by for a go-around. We always parted company with the same closing, the best compliment we knew how to give each other, "You gave me something to think about." Denton's been gone for a number of years now, and I'm still reflecting on things he gave me to think about.

I didn't have a restroom in my little shop on Main Street so I used the women's room for the offices located above the theatre. The stairwell door was self-closing, but loudly slammed when it closed, so folks upstairs always knew when someone was on their way up. The theatre employees must have been working on some kind of project when I slammed my way up the stairs one day because when I got to the top the manager asked, from her office, which did not give her a view of the stairs, "Do you need my help?" I poked my head in her door and said, "Thanks, but I've been managing to go to the restroom on my own for a number of years now." The next day, that very nice lady with a very understated sense of humor saw me heading up from the street and she said, "Really, just let me know if you need any help. I'm here for you." And, she really was! Shortly after that, the theater put in toilet paper dispensers that were huge rolls, locked in, in the office restrooms to replace what had been the kind you'd have in your house. I wasn't exactly sure how I was going to borrow the men's room roll when the women's was running low, once playing hide and seek the toilet paper... women's room to men's room to women's room... was no longer possible but she solved that for me. I went up one day and I found a small roll of toilet paper with this note attached, "Sorry Roxanne. Toilet paper theft. We will replace it as soon as the order comes in. I blame 10 plus sold-out shows!" There's thoughtful, and then there's making sure there's more toilet paper on the roll than what you'd leave when you're trying to get the next person to change it thoughtful. Next level, that!

When Mormons cross paths with Catholic children: I was out on the sidewalk yakking with a city worker when a trio of young Latter Day Saints on a mission stopped and introduced themselves, with "Sister" before their names, and then asked to have a few inspirational words with us. Me, "Nice to meet you. No, you don't need to talk to me. I'm well covered in the inspirational sister department since I have five of my own." (I'm the sixth of six daughters in my family.) The speaker looked at me like, "What?" then turned and looked at the city worker and he said, "I've got six." They left, with a bit of a wrinkle to their brows. Going with the odds, I turned and asked the city worker, "Catholic?" Yep.

<<<<<>>>>>

In the world of really cool stuff that happens in small towns? A lot of people say they'd like to go out with a bang but thus far, I only know of one who really did. There was a rather courtly elder man who used to make the rounds of the businesses every year, collecting for the 4th of July fireworks. He was always nattily dressed, in a place where high fashion is clean boots, and always of a dignified demeanor. I especially appreciated him after I asked him one year why it was that when Independence Day fell on a Sunday, the fireworks were shot off on the Saturday before. He told me it was at the request of the churches at the time they established the fireworks committee (in the 1960s) so that the celebrations would not interfere with church services. I asked, "Does that seem right to you? Changing the date for churches when, without the First Amendment, their freedom to conduct services at all could have been problematic? And really, the 4th of July is the only holiday with the date built right into the name." He said he'd look into it, and he did, and since that time the 4th of July has been celebrated on the 4th of July. It just so happened that at the time he died, our fireworks aficionado was also our undertaker, and as I heard it, he undertook to make sure that the dapper gentleman gave us one last show of class: by having a bit of his ashes placed in a projectile that exploded in a shower of beauty. Such a fitting last act for that lovely man.

Those, "Look at me go!" moments: In a not-unusual occurrence, some tourists stopped in to ask for directions, which I gave them, to include distance, even though I never actually know how far anything is so, I would just make it up. (I learned over many years that people always asked, before and after GPS since we were an "unknown destination"

for quite a while after it was introduced, and were then disturbed if you didn't know the distance. However, I also knew they'd find whatever they were looking for, since it's a small town, so I started giving people my made-up distances under the theory that they didn't actually know what a mile feels like anyway, coming in from kilometer world, and it gave them confidence when maneuvering a foreign nation. Even better, just to solidify that confidence, I always gave them decimal points: 1.2 miles or the like.) When I told Marty about it later he thought I was off on the distance so we made a bet and drove it to check and–ON THE NOSE! The exact distance I made up! Uh-huh, I'm just that good at lying! Uh, I mean…

Don't you just hate it when you're standing around, minding your own business, and you feel a bug crawling on you and all your efforts to unobtrusively dislodge it fail so you start doing the "Spider Dance" (swiping madly all over your person, sure now that it's a tarantula or something equally terrifying)... only to find that it's a hair you shed on yourself? Do it on a Main Street, and your neighbor just might give you a dollar for the performance, all while snickering away.

I had a man come into my shop one day and we got into talking about how one might amuse oneself on a slow day and at that moment, a mouse quite obligingly ran down the street, with a broom-wielding person on its tail. Then a young guy took a bag of popcorn out of the trash can out front and walked off eating it. Nothing like a demonstration to show that there's no end to how one might amuse oneself on a slow day.

In small-town news: The FedEx guy who does the Main Street route also does the residential route sometimes. Because I collected packages for the theatre when they were closed I would see drivers regularly downtown but not often at home since I rarely received packages there. A new driver came onto the downtown route who then ended up delivering a package at my house. When I answered the doorbell, I saw him getting back in his van and waved and yelled, "Hey! How ya doing?" He squinted at me until he was able to place me and then said, "Roxanne? What are you doing here?" Me, "I live here." FedEx guy, "Oh." (Like it never occurred to him that I live somewhere. Just like the first time you see one of your teachers in public and realize they're a person, and not a classroom fixture, I was the "bookstore lady" meant to always be in my shop.)

When you walk back and forth to work every day (which I did, having never had a driver's license) you get really good at making eye contact with drivers to make sure they see you. However, there is nothing you can do about someone coming up fast from behind and straight into the turn except be grateful that their engine was loud enough to provide warning. If only someone had been timing me when I went from a casual walk to mach speed one day to avoid being mowed over by a driver who never did see me, I might have been offered a spot on the Olympic team. I mean really, I hadn't run that fast since I was a teenager running from the poli... uh, never mind.

From Wild West to Wild Kingdom going on in front of my shop, some days. Like a sparrow and a moth fighting it out and frankly, I wasn't sure at first who was going to win but, the beak carried the day. No need to wonder about who the locals would have been rooting for, as evidenced by the big pick-up truck parked in front of my place one day that was honoring miller moth season by having wired a big ex-butterfly-yard-ornament-faded-to-look-like-a-moth to the front grille. *SPLAT*

It was on Main Street that I learned one of the major differences between how rural people and city people use an SUV. Yep, saw a city person in an SUV, that clearly said "off-road" on the side, rolling their tires on the sidewalk in an attempt to parallel park. Definitely off-roading, there!

During the bookstore years I had some really interesting requests by mail, but only one meant to foster international relations. I got a letter from a guy in Utah looking for used Latvian language CDs so he could be more "proactive" in his "long-distance courtship." Must come cheap because, "You see, I don't have a lot of money because of my incarceration." Don't know about you, but I'm guessing there was more court involved in that courting than the woman probably knew.

My neighbor, "Love your kicks!" Me, looking down at my feet, "Well, dang! I was so distracted this morning I wore my good sneakers to work. Now that witch I work for will probably expect me to dress up every day."

Odd–but nice! For no apparent reason, my computer interrupted my data input to ask me if I wanted "sticky keys." Well hmmm... I did often have sticky keys, the result of chocolate and peanut butter but I did not on that day, so I took it to mean it was time to go next door to the theatre and get a Reese's. Really, what's not to love about a computer that looks out for your chocolate habit that way?

There's a ledge below my display window at the shop that people often sat on that had two kids (maybe ten and twelve) lounging on it when I got to work. I wasn't moving very fast that day, so I went inside and cranked up the sounds to help kick in some motivation. After a few minutes the kids came into the shop and one said (with a put-upon sigh, like I was assaulting the ears they had parked on my window sill), "You listen to the same music as my grandparents." I had to suppress a laugh so I could look at them straight-faced and ask, "You meant to say I rock out to the same tunes as your grandparents, right?" The kids both looked at me like, well, the way kids look at you when they can't decide if you're joking or just plain nuts and said, "Uh-huh." No taste in music aside, I'm hoping they grow up to be like the new FedEx guy who came in when the sun peeked out after a number of gray days. You know that just brings happy with it so yeah, it was a beautiful day on Main Street that caused me to be rockin' the tunes at a volume that drowned out the bell on the door, and so it was that the first time I met him he totally caught me dancing and singing in the bookstore. Did he laugh? Well, maybe just a little. But then in the manner of awesome people everywhere, he felt the funk and moved to the groove. American Bandstand woulda had nothin' on us, I'm tellin' ya, if not for my grandfathered-in inward-opening door that brought a rather abrupt halt to the driver's attempt to glide right out it. (Smack!) Major points for the quick recovery and courtly bow out, though.

We used to have a stone monument at the edge of town, in the cemetery, that said, "Welcome to Cortez." I couldn't begin to count how many tourists, over the years, asked about it. They always wondered if there was any special reason it was sitting in the cemetery–and I always left that up to them to decide. (It was eventually turned into a veteran's memorial, and I can see why but still, I've always rather missed its old incarnation.)

It is my understanding that in my bookstore years, Cortez lost an average of three citizens a year to a combination of alcoholism and exposure. Those of us who owned Main Street shops tended to have a significant amount of contact with the homeless community, as it was not unusual for folks to wander downtown. My Dad, who often covered the shop for me, was in the bookstore one day with a homeless man who'd come by for books we'd give him when a woman (by resemblance maybe a sister, maybe a niece) came in. The woman reached up to straighten the man's collar, wrapped a few bills in his hand, gripped his arm tightly, then turned and left. All in silence. One of the most moving displays of unconditional love my Dad had ever witnessed. Sadly, that gentleman would become one of the three lost over that winter.

Have you ever thought about how you might get around if you lost your driver's license for some reason and lived in a place with no bus and limited taxi service? (For many years Cortez had one "cab", when the car owner felt like driving. Uber, before Uber.) Well, wonder no more! Folks in Cortez have solved that problem for you. Just hop on your riding lawn mower and cut a swatch through town. Supposed to pick up a few friends? No problem, just attach a wagon on the back for those carpool days. Or maybe it's just that you're tired of traffic and wish you could get a little breathing room from all the other vehicles? Well, listen up, then! It's simple: just get behind the wheel of a big rig with "student driver" signs plastered all over it. Worked great for the one I saw one day.

No! Us, a fast-food, instant-gratification kind of society?! Not so! BUT, if for some reason you are unable to get to church on Ash Wednesday, not to worry, Cortezians have got you covered. Two ministers with a cross, an ash jar and a sign saying "Ashes to Go" can be found cruising Main Street for your convenience.

Never let it be said that Cortez is not populated by law-abiding citizens. Leash law in your town? And your well-trained dog is taking exception? No problem, just put a leash on him and drape it across his back. (Nothing says you have to be holding it, right?) Now, your goat, on the other hand, they must need the leash in hand; leastwise the one strolling around downtown had one.

Got a call from "John Kennedy" one day, telling me that he works for UPS and had a package of mine for two days that he needed to discuss with me. I said, "Really, what's to discuss? Put it on a brown truck and send it my way. Isn't that what you do?" He tried to add some more drivel so I said, "Yes, there is commonly free produce on Main Street (we are indeed one of those towns where if you have a pick-up or don't lock your doors, folks will drop their excess garden harvest on you), but that doesn't mean I just fell off the turnip truck so no, I'm not paying you for a package that just 'turned-up.' "

I had a day where it was just bugging me that I could not remember the UPS guy's name. The mail carrier was Mike. The FedEx guy was Mike. Well, not really, he was James, but went by Mike. Then I thought, "Ooohhh, that'd be awfully convenient if the UPS guy was Mike, too! I wonder if he'd be willing to go by Mike, whatever his name really is? Or maybe he is Mike... and goes by James." And then I was just confused, and wishing the theatre carried Mike and Ike's.

For the "Hitchhiker's Guide to Travel." (Not that I'm advocating hitchhiking, mind you, but if you're going to do it anyway.) First rule of thumb: establish that the person you are trying to hitch a ride from actually has a ride. You know, a car, motorcycle, bicycle, horse, little red wagon, travois... something. Yep, I was walking home one night and had someone ask me if I was going *finger point* that way. I said yes. (Pointedly looking down at my feet, which had been working a certain alternating pattern where one went in front of the other... heading in that direction.) Then the person asked if I would give them a ride. Since I was pretty sure trying a piggy-back ride for someone quite a bit taller and heavier than I was would have landed us both in the gutter, I had to politely decline. Now, can I get a thumb's up for exercising my common sense and not picking up a hitchhiker?

A lick and a promise! I was watching a family walk down the street, the Mom holding one kid in one arm, the other by the hand, and a big pupper on a leash. The toddler guy decided he wanted to walk on his own so the Mom let go of his hand and he sped up till he was right behind the pupper. Then the big pupper's big tail wagged and wiped out little toddling guy. Little toddling guy started sobbing, loudly. Big pupper turned around, planted himself on the sidewalk next to the little toddler guy and started licking toddler's face until the little guy was helplessly laughing. And there are folks out there who think kissing it doesn't make it better. Pshaw!

As a service to the community, the theatre runs a "Free Movie Tuesdays Summer Kids Series" throughout the summer months. A very much appreciated service if the number of parents who shoved their kids out of their cars and drove off as if, well, school had already been out for a week, was any indication. And, if I'm any kind of judge, very much missed when the season was over but the kids were not yet back in school. My first clue? When I overheard a kid tell their Mom that there wasn't a free movie and the Mom made the kid go back and double-check. Second clue? When the Mom said, "I don't have enough cash on me for popcorn and the movie but you're going anyway." Kid, "Can I at least look for change in the car?" Mom, "You got five minutes. Good luck." For me, Free Movie Tuesday was invariably followed by Window Washing Wednesday, which was all about trying to think of a way to turn all the tiny, buttery, post-Tuesday handprints on the bottom of my glass door into an advertising lure. Like, maybe add some sodium chloride and call it a salt-lick station for people's puppers? A thought. But then, what to do about the kids that would end up licking it? And then, when the season was over, it was all about trying to figure out some way to decorate the door of my shop, once I would no longer have the "small person hanging off the door bar" decorations to look at every Tuesday.

You know, there are still people out there who try to claim that machines don't have minds of their own, don't play pranks on folks. But there are those of us who know better. I was walking to work one day and a city worker was on a big riding mower, mowing down the grass between the sidewalk and street. He kindly turned the mower off so I could pass without getting hit by all the debris, so I slowed when I reached him to say thank you, and the mower belched and shot dirt right at me. I said to the city worker, "Well, glad it enjoyed its breakfast." When I was walking away, I heard the city worker say to the mower, "Now, why'd you go and do that to the nice lady?" And I swear, that mower laughed.

People can be so cool! We had a really hot summer with a lot of reports of people suffering from heat exhaustion. During that summer, I left my house one morning and was about half a block away when a lady (a stranger to me) who had just turned the corner stopped to offer me a ride. I told her I really appreciated the offer but I was good. She asked, "Are you sure? You look hot." I was thinking to myself, "How can that be possible? I just walked out of air-conditioning like twenty steps ago." And then the light went on so I said, "Thank you so much. I'm not actually sweating, my hair is still a bit damp from my shower. But how thoughtful of you to be concerned." Made my day! Kindness is always chill.

I am admittedly a person of some odd habits but I didn't know that not actually being at the bookstore when it was closed was considered one of them until someone called me at home (that's what you get when you use your husband's unusual last name in the shop name, easy phone-book access to your home number) to ask me if I realized my shop was closed. Well, yeah, I kind of knew it was going to be when I put up the sign saying, "Closed until Jan 5th."

I did not fully appreciate just how many Cortezians got to know our dog Happy through the "Happy Tales" columns that she wrote (with a little help from me and her Grandpa) and that Gail ran in the Four Corners Free Press, until after I put up a sign, "Closed due to Happy's illness." When I reopened, folks I'd never seen before came in the bookstore (cautiously, in case it was bad news) to ask how she was doing. I finally got a clue and put up a "Happy is doing well!" sign. Then folks came in with big smiles. Nice.

I had a gentleman in the bookstore one day who (bless his heart) theorized that the reason I am a (self-described) black thumb when it comes to gardening is that I don't talk to the plants enough. Maybe the only person in my life who ever proposed that I don't talk enough.

There was a devil on my shoulder some days but really, sometimes folks just make it too tempting to resist. First up: a lady asked for a book recommendation, then noticed the Four Corners Free Press stand and pointed out to me that the Free Press cost 50 cents, which means it isn't free. So, I recommended a dictionary. Second up: A guy came in asking for a recommendation for "A good book, something interesting." I had to say, "Finally! Someone NOT looking for boring and stupid…"

I had a young guy in the bookstore one day picking up books for what he told me was his upcoming twelve-day stint in jail. He rode his bike up, so I asked that he not ride it away. He said, as so many do, that Main Street is not safe to ride on. I agreed, and included the sidewalk as unsafe for pedestrians due to bikes. I asked him to imagine that he mowed over my Mom, who had young-onset Parkinson's disease. Then he, unlike so many, said, "I would feel terrible if that happened!" and walked his bike away. My thanks to him.

Me to my neighbor, when talking about the upcoming holidays, "Can you believe it? That witch I work for gave me a Christmas bonus!" My neighbor, "Nice! What are you going to buy with it?" Me, "Something for her, apparently, since, of course, she followed it up with a wish list of things for me to buy her but hey, baby steps. I'm still shocked she's giving me any time off since you know her, if she's here, she expects me to be, too."

They say it takes some time to be recognized by other business owners when you open your own. I'm thinking when a fellow business owner takes time out of their day to walk down from their shop to yours and give you a "slug bug" over the VW parked across the street (a la the kids' road trip game.), you are all the way there. That was the start of the slug bug wars downtown. Many participated, and even though some had an unfair advantage because an unwritten rule was not popping someone on a new tattoo (or even a fake new tattoo. What, I was supposed to just give them an edge?), that shop owner still proved out as the most accomplished. I never quite reached her level; however, I did make good use of diversionary tactics once by contending that "bug slug" is right and proper (see the bug, then slug. Bug slugged. Bug slugging), even though I knew it's not, and got my best shot in while the debate was raging over that.

Sometimes you just gotta draw boundaries with the people around you. Me to a theatre employee, "You know, you'd think someone who has pierced everything they can think of and has multiple tattoos–and who doesn't like it when people comment on them–would leave the paper cut on my face unremarked." (I mean, really, how did they think I got it? Doing something smart?)

When I opened the bookstore, I was totally clueless about anything having to do with running my own business and was particularly concerned that I get the sales tax right since I didn't want to tangle with the government, but found the small business info I got from the state distinctly unhelpful on that front, so I went into the city offices and asked for a "practice form." The look on the lady's face! I said, "I'm going have to sign these forms under all sorts of threats about what you will do to me if I get it wrong (but, no pressure, right?) and I didn't wake up this morning just knowing how to do it right, so I could use some help." That hit some kind of nerve for her, made her laugh, and she decided on the spot to do a "fake" form with me. Book learnin'–it can only take you so far.

And the attempted guilt trip, uh, rather, sales pitch of the day went to: the Durango spa package sales guy! (Even if he was trying to convince me that MY math was off when I pointed out that a fifty-dollar discount is not ninety percent off of three-hundred-fifty dollars.) I just don't think you can find anyone less patient with folks selling "deals" to Durango businesses than a small business owner in Cortez. (We're rather their poor relations.) After a hard sell I told him it's too bad for him that I'm not really the spa type but that even if I was, I'd be spending that money more locally, so better luck elsewhere. And he said, "Oh, it's fine, my kids can eat Top Ramen another few days." Ever helpful, I gave him ideas for what he could add to it. (Yes, I once lived in a dorm. Ha!)

I really am just that kind of annoying. I had a young man in the shop (maybe fifteen or sixteen), selling over-priced food stuff from a catalog that I didn't want and didn't need, in order to raise money for a farm/ranch-related trip to Denver. Me being the now grown me who still remembers my first foray into sales I knew I was going to give him the money (I always did–without requiring anyone cry) but still asked all sorts of questions about the trip, and learned that the bottom line for him was excitement about what he would learn. After he got done explaining it all to me I told him, "I don't want or need what's being sold here but I'll give you the cash for one item and you can do with it what you want." He said, "You can't give me the money now, not until you get the item." I said, "I'm giving it to you now, and you now have a decision to make: you can keep the cash and just spend it, you can use it directly for the trip, you can buy an item with the cash and donate it, you can buy an item and eat it yourself, you could keep some of it and donate some of it. All sorts of options." He said, "But how will you know what I do with it?" I said, "I won't. But you will. Consider this your first trip-related lesson." He had no idea how to take that, but I had hope he'd figure it out.

One of the conveniences of having a theatre next door was that I would sometimes go by there and buy candy in order to fix the cash in my till. (Totally true! Is it my fault that all they were selling to the general public was junk food?) I went by one day but they claimed a change imbalance themselves and gave me a roll of dimes. Say what?! Me, "I see how you are, diming me out to that witch I work for, for getting candy on her dime. Sheesh!"

Dealing with tax stuff for the bookstore made me wholly appreciate when the city official came by and looked at my shop for the purpose of evaluating personal property taxes and said, "'Yeah, you don't need to file, there's no measurable value here," and I just looked around and smiled, because they were right, the value of books is totally immeasurable.

And then came the day that I learned I had apparently come up with a really sneaky way of encouraging repeat business, and didn't even know it. Had an elder gentleman in the bookstore who was so outraged that his favorite author was in the "Romance" section that he vowed to come back to identify each author that I had "mis-shelved." And so he did, and bought more books while he was at it.

I always so enjoyed all those people who just walked in my door and set themselves up for my brand of teasing. I had a couple from Missouri complaining about the airport scanners and searches. (A bit of a strip and pat down for the husband.) Really, how does one resist asking how folks from "The Show Me State" could object to, well, a little showing? Especially when they just had to end their complaint by saying, "Ya feel me?"

Ah, the smell of campfire in your hair. Every year, we'd have a little pit fire for my defunct shop paperwork and burn all the evidence. Uh, I mean the paper-trail. No, the documents! (That's why my Dad, the retired CPA, always told me that if I were ever audited I would need to just shut up. Me, "What? They're all proper and accurate words. Can I help it if people put incorrect connotations on them?" My Dad, "You will if you don't want to be arrested.")

I generally suck at remembering names and faces but people's stories? Not bad at that one. I had a gentleman in I hadn't seen in years; didn't recognize him and his name didn't ring a bell, but the minute he reminded me of his business in Ohio I knew where his kid worked and his favorite authors. And I'm sure it had absolutely nothing to do with the fact that his business in Ohio was: a candy store.

When we were kids and called each other names my folks made us define the word we were using. If we could not do so adequately, they made us look it up. (Under the theory that you ought to know what it means when you call somebody something.) Which is why I was thinking, on the day a guy in the shop called me an "intelligentsia" (not as a compliment) that he would have benefited from that approach. (For my part, I just kept giving him reasons to repeat it... cuz I'm just a glutton for punishment.)

I maintained a strict policy from day one at the bookstore: If you really want a book but are short on funds, take it, settle up with me later. And yes, some folks never did settle up. However, it mattered not to me, since the moments like the one I had, where a young man came back a year later to settle up and thank me for the trust; those moments were not about money.

I had a customer one day who was a self-described cantankerous old guy from New Jersey. Then he gave me a two-dollar bill and after I told him the last one I saw was the one Marty brought half of to Germany when he was stationed there that we reunited when he got home, I saw his cantankerous old heart melt and right before my eyes he turned into a sentimental old guy from New Jersey. Then he asked where we keep it and I said, "Oh, we spent it years ago" and cantankerous old guy from New Jersey was back, looking ready to throttle me. (What can you do? We were poor college students at the time, and practicality outweighed sentimentality.) It mollified him a bit when I pointed out that once the bill was re-joined we set it free to pursue its own destiny but still, all apologies to whoever waited on him that night at the restaurant he was heading for. Pretty sure they didn't get a two-dollar bill but did get to meet the once-again cantankerous old guy from New Jersey.

I used to think about people by genre in the bookstore but I can't recall ever having said it aloud until I ran into a young man who said, "I know you! Where do I know you from? Oh yeah, the bookstore!" Me, taking a closer look at him, "Yes, you're Fantasy! With a little bit of Mystery." He just busted up! Said he was happy to be a fantasy with a bit of mystery to him, so happy he might have to tell that to future dates.

Me, in response to a situation Marty had at work, "I'll bet you were thinking, 'What the hell?!'" Marty, "Exactly! Except, I only swear to myself in abbreviations at work (WTH?!) because I'm polite and thinking the actual words would just be rude." Me, "Huh. That witch I work for never worries about that."

The secret life of the FedEx guy! (Who though his Southern accent was pretty much gone, still had a slower, drawn-out speech rhythm, so read this with that in mind): "You don't watch Hannibal, do you?" Me, "No, but I read the books." Him, "Well, they have recipes on the show so my wife and I decided to try one. Google it, you'll see. Couldn't do many of them because we just don't have those kind of ingredients here and really, most are ingredients you wouldn't want to eat but, we found one to try. Had to buy a bottle of Port to make it so I was explaining to the guy I bought the Port from what we were doing and his eyes just got bigger and bigger. So I told him, 'Oh, it's okay, we found a pork loin to substitute for the human leg' and he said, 'Oh, good to hear.' It was good! Google it, you'll see." Me, "Uh-huh. You know that if you ever invite us to dinner we're eating out, right?" He laughed. I said, "And you know I'm going to be telling this story all week." He said, "Oh yeah, tell everyone to Google it... it was good!" So, there ya go... Google it!

So, I was looking down the street at the chalkboard sidewalk sign in front of my neighbor's business, trying to figure out why it said, "EAR

23

OPEN"... then took my sunglasses off... and realized it said, "BAR OPEN." Then I had to wonder if I should wash my sunglasses or accept that a worker's fairy has given me the ability to see the truth under the advertising. Bartenders: the underpaid listeners of the world.

I screwed up once and inadvertently paid my state retail sales taxes to the city and the city taxes to the state. It was those kind of moments that made me think I ought to have gone into government or big business, where people are so commonly promoted for such errors; with better hours and better pay, just to get them out of the way. I could so totally have been incompetent enough for that. But noooo, I had to go for small business, and whenever I screwed up, that witch I worked for made me stay late and fix it – without pay!

A very endearing story: When I first opened the bookstore, my next-door neighbor was a thrift store staffed by adults who were cognitively disabled. Many of the employees who worked there would come over and visit with me on their breaks. A few months after it closed one of the gentlemen who used to come by came in and told me about his new job; the hours he worked and the pay he received. He then showed me his Special Olympics medals and told me about the land he would inherit. And then told me he had decided it was time to marry. I congratulated him on his accomplishments and wished him luck in his marriage, adding that I have been married for many years and highly recommend it. He exclaimed, "You're married?!" and then scooped up his medals, and abruptly left. I tried to catch him so I could try to understand what had upset him but he wasn't having any of that. He did not come into the bookstore again for quite a while. When he did finally come in again, he told me that he had decided that we could still be friends, even though he had intended to ask me on a date before I hurt his feelings by telling him I was married. He told me all the things he had planned for our first date, and how disappointed he had been that we couldn't do them. (I told him that they were all wonderful ideas that the right young lady, when he met her, would really enjoy.) A few months later, he came in to tell me Happy Valentine's Day. He told me that he wanted me to understand that it was a gesture from one friend to another, that he had no intentions besides simply letting me know he appreciated me as a friend. He then came by regularly again, just to say hello, and always brought a smile for me with him.

It's a competitive world out there! A delivery driver pulled up close to the curb at a spot on Main where the sidewalk was all broken. I said to him, when he came in, "Good thing you were back just a bit from the bricks, they popped a driver's tire a few weeks ago and since drivers can't change the tires, he was stuck here for a while." Driver, "Amateur! I run over curbs all the time without popping a tire. Who'd he drive for?" Me, "Same company as you." "Ohhhhh! You just made my day! Can't wait to get back to the distribution center…"

Sidewalk test, an efficient means of finding out who your friends are (or even just helpful strangers). I was getting ready to walk by a couple of young guys on one of the pedestrian-unfriendly streets of Cortez, moving at a pretty good clip, and veered a bit to the right to give them a little more room; stepped on a crack and... hello pavement! (My Mom's back was fine. No ill-effects from me stepping on that crack. But thank you for thinking of her.) Had they been the type with reflexes (I was going to say quick reflexes but really, quick wasn't required, just any at all, seeing as how I was really close to catching myself) they might have saved me the spill, but no such luck. Then they just stood there looking at me so I said, "Everyone loves taking a fall with an audience, especially such a helpful one. No, no, no need to ask me if I'd like a hand up, I'm obviously a well-coordinated person and since it looks like nothing's broken, I'll be fine." (They were totally looking at me like I was a movie they were watching or something.) So, like humans are prone to do, I showed off my scraped palm to my neighbors (I don't know what it is about showing it off that makes it feel better, but undeniably true) and telling them the story. They all told me they'd have tried to catch me and if they missed they'd have offered me a hand up, but they'd have been sad to miss out on my monologue.

People are so funny! Had a guy park his truck in front of the shop, one pupper riding shotgun, one in the center of the backseat. After he left the vehicle, the passenger pupper moved to the driver's seat and the backseat pupper took shotgun. When the man came back I said, "So, looks like it's Red's (it was a red pupper) turn to drive, Black and White's turn to pick the music, and you get the backseat." He laughed and said, "Nah. The deal is one gets the front coming, the other gets it going, and they get to drive when I'm drunk. So far, they haven't figured out whether they're coming or going and I don't drink."

Seriously?! I was walking to work one day and I was about a quarter of the way into crossing the street at the Post Office when a car came barreling toward me. I did a "Really?!" gesture and they stopped and then the driver yelled out the window at me, "That is not a crosswalk." Me, "It is a crosswalk, and I have the right of way." Driver, "There are no lines." (It was recently patched, and no lines laid down yet, but whatever, didn't change the situation.) Me, "Do I need to get someone from the Post Office to explain it to you?" (Postal carriers, they deal with mean dogs, so right up their alley.)

One thing I definitely should have done when I first opened my shop was start keeping a tally of how many vehicle "incidents" I saw over the years. (I doubt folks are really aware of just how often, when they are parallel parked, their bumpers have been tapped, rolled over, etc.) One day it was a back bumper on truck rolling over the front bumper on car. I'd probably not have noticed but the car's license plate got stuck under the truck and the car was rocking so hard from the truck driver trying to separate them that I caught it out of the side of my eye and thought it was hydraulics, right up until my rational mind kicked in enough to wonder why anyone would put hydraulics on a sub-compact. It's pretty surprising to me that I only once ever ended up speaking to a cop about something I witnessed. It was a totally freak occurrence where I walked an elder lady down the street to her car with the books she'd bought and was just heading back through my doorway when I saw the vehicle fly across the street (hit nothing, amazing) and then fly right back toward me. I beelined for the back of the bookstore, so I missed the part where she managed to yank the wheel hard enough to only take out the secured flower pot and parking sign in front of the theatre. The cop was a little testy, that my eye-witness account wasn't what he hoped for until I said, "Come on! An attitude? I was putting as much real estate between me and that car as I could get." He laughed, said he guessed that's what he'd have been doing, too.

Oh yes, there are angels among us. I walked the same route to my shop for many years, and I often crossed paths with the same people; one of them a gentleman who was not "all there" but always friendly, and always had a smile for me, though we never had a conversation. I didn't know his name, and he didn't know mine. He would greet me by using a variety of endearments. One day, when I was dispirited from a Parkinson's-related medical emergency for my Mom, he greeted me by saying, "Good Morning, Beautiful." I said, "Good Morning. And thank you. A nice thing to hear, as I am not feeling at my best today." He said, "Oh, you can't not be beautiful, you wear your heart on your face." And then he just turned and went, leaving me with a lightened spirit. An angel, indeed.

You never have to worry if your phone will ever ring in a small shop because it's definitely going to, often with folks representing themselves as your phone company wanting to give you a great deal. So I'd say, "Great, give me the phone number and I'll call back as soon as I have a minute." To which they'd reply, "We don't have a phone number for you to call." I'd say, "You don't have a phone number for me to call?" They'd say, "No, we don't." Me, "Still want to stick with your story? That you represent my phone company, and want to give me a better deal, BUT YOU DON'T HAVE A PHONE NUMBER?" Then they'd hang up on me, and my day would be complete.

Unless I get a ride I walk everywhere I go, and since either circumstance causes me to carry on my person the things most would leave in their car, I often have people looking at my backpack like they are wondering why I lugged it in with me, and some who find a sideways way to ask. I walked to an appointment and a lady in the waiting area said, "Did you walk? It's hot out there for a walk" Me (with a smile), "Do I look that sweaty? I don't drive, so walking it is." Lady, "You never drive?" Me, "Nope, never had a driver's license." She said, "You're only the second person I've ever met who never had a license!" Me, "Where'd you meet the first one?" Lady, "At a bookstore on Main Street many years ago." I chuckled. Lady, "Oh my God, that was you, wasn't it?!" Me, "Uh-huh. I get around, even without a car."

What's not to love about bureaucracies? When I opened my business account at the bank I had to give them a one-hundred-dollar deposit for an account that required no minimum balance. I asked, "So, now that the account is open I could just take the hundred bucks back out?" "Yes." And folks say these types of things with a straight face, and then look puzzled when you roll your eyes and laugh. Huh.

That happy-as-a-kid moment when: you saw the theatre manager chase the FedEx guy down the street to give him a movie poster he had admired when the movie was playing and the FedEx guy lit up like a Christmas tree and asked, "Really?! I can have it?"

Do I think I can dance? Well, yeah! In fact, I'm an accomplished sidewalk dancer. Heck, in one week alone I two-stepped with someone I was trying to pass on my way to work, square-danced with a bearded fellow outside the bank door, slam-danced with a kid running down the street, and tangoed with a lady who backed in to me in front of the shop. (And wow, did she ever manage a low dip before I pulled her back up.) And I definitely have the scars on my hands to prove what a great break-dancer I am.

Now me? Had I had a hold function on my phone at the bookstore I wouldn't have played elevator music, I'd have played the Twilight Zone theme music. Then solicitors could have spent their wait time wondering if the call was really worth being all alone with endless books and broken reading glasses.

We all know that the way to get rid of a song, or a phrase, or whatever earworm that is stuck in your head is to give it away. (Right?) Well, one way to deal with a boring day is to pump it up a notch and see if you can make it go viral. I had the bulk of Main Street saying, "It's Shake 'n Bake and I heeeeeelped" one day. You know you've achieved your goal when you run into the spouse of a fellow business owner the next day and they say it to you.

Best ad ever for a movie? One of the theatre folks came by to tell me to come meet the newest theatre denizen: a bat hanging out by the exit door. While we were out there a family parked their car, got out, and then the dad slammed his finger in the door. It was a pretty bad slam; he was hopping all over the place while the blood was flowing. I went and got him a wet paper towel and returned just in time to hear the Mom, "Is it broken? No? Then use the paper towel, and here's a Band-

Aid. We're not missing this movie and a couple of hours with grateful kids glued to a screen over a little blood."

Yes, yes, I was the mean shop lady who pointed out to people that wanted to hang their fliers or posters in my window that they either needed to be using painters tape or agree to come back and scrape off that Scotch tape. For those who argued that Scotch is not that difficult to take off (and trust me, they did), I offered an experiment, "Let's stick them both on the hairiest part of your arm." I used my own painter's tape to put it up the first time, and they always showed up with painter's tape the next.

So, these were the rules (and there was no rule requiring that you be made aware of the rules): If you came into my shop trying to sell me something, asked for my name, and then sang Roxanne back to me (a la The Police song.) you had just solicited me to: screw with you. I asked one guy who sang my name to me where he was from and he said, "One of my driver's licenses is Durango." I asked, "One of them? Where are the others from? And what's your name on them? I bet it's John." He said, "No, it's the latest..." and I interrupted, "One in your collection? How many you got? Are you a prepper? Or just a criminal?" That must have stung, since you'd have thought the cops were on his tail by the speed with which he left.

There are people out there who might argue that we are not, like the sign says, the friendliest town in the Southwest; however, they must be people who never blew Marty a kiss after he dropped them off at work and had both Marty and the stranger in the car next to him blow one back.

And, there's a skill set I definitely don't have! A lady walked down the street one day, eating, with a cup balanced on her head that she took down to drink from, then put back. She was walking at a good clip, too. Chewing-gum-and-walking people may now bow to her.

We had such a full-service situation on Main Street, you could even get a heart check. I was unlocking my shop one day and saw two probably nine-year-old boys reflected in the glass. I turned just as one darted across the center of the street to the other side. The other hesitated at the front corner of a large SUV, and then decided to go. He didn't see the traffic just released from the red light moving toward him so I yelled at him to stop, and he jumped back behind the vehicle. He just made it, but might not have if not for the wholly impressive reaction time of the lady who literally stood on her brakes to avoid hitting him. A split second slower on any of our parts, and I'd hate to think. And I learned that yes, your heart can jump into your throat and you can still speak while it's there because when the kid then said, "I think it's better if I walk to the corner and cross at the light," I managed to say, "Ya think?"

I had a visit one day at the bookstore from an elder gentleman that I volunteered with when we first moved to Cortez. I had been the youngest volunteer at the establishment by a good thirty-five years, and was significantly more outspoken than my elders. He came by just to reassure me that he hadn't cleaned a toilet at the place where we volunteered ever since I uttered the words to the paid administrator at my first staff meeting that started the "elder revolt": "You aren't seriously telling me that the RETIRED VOLUNTEERS are expected to clean the toilets when you are cashing a paycheck, are you?" Laughed till he cried, and totally made my day.

Life in the sole-proprietor lane: I made an executive decision at the shop one day. I did that sometimes. And somehow, they always meant more work for me that was not originally in my job description, so the file of complaints I wrote about that witch I worked for? Huge!

Rodeo Week is a big deal in Cortez. It had been running for almost seventy years straight when I opened the bookstore and is still running today. We had friends who ran the mutton bustin' and stick-horse races, so my shop bought all the bubblegum they distributed to the kids for those events. We even had a "sheriff" go around and ticket business owners (as a charitable fundraiser.) if they weren't dressed for the occasion. And though I always donated to the fundraiser; after receiving a ticket my first year, I was all in for dressing for Rodeo Week every subsequent year. I'd wear a cowboy hat, cowboy boots, a bandana, and blue jeans–then eat too much the weekend before so that my jeans would be too tight.

I can't say I'd ever previously spent much time thinking about how much of the quality of life is defined by restrooms (mostly just on road trips) but I was thinking about it the day when my fellow theatre tenant told me we were under new management and, "So far it's all good, there are even hand-drying towels in the restrooms, now." (Whoohoo!) Yep, we could overlook a lot of things with the less diligent, but drying our hands on our pants was just a little too gas-stationy.

It wasn't really fun being a bookstore during flu season. People would stop to buy books because they were sick and knew they were going to go down hard. I finally had to put up a sign that said, "When stopping to buy a book because you are sick and want something to read in bed please do not breathe on the nice book lady, do not sneeze on the nice book lady, and definitely DO NOT wipe your nose with your hand and then use that hand to try and hand money to the nice book lady.

Voluntary compliance with this directive is appreciated. Non-compliance with this directive will result in any illness contracted from you being named for you." Gave some folks a laugh before they were going to be miserable, anyway.

Looking literally at Main Street I observed, daily, that given three empty parallel parking spots in a row folks invariably parked in the middle one, forcing other drivers to parallel park and granting me a view of the varying levels of competence. I seriously thought about making up ribbons to hand out. "The good" (got it first time), "the bad" (extra maneuvering required), "the ugly" (curb climbers), and the participation ribbon "Got your license out of a Cracker Jack box, didn't ya?"

Retail 101: Business tends to be brisker when you remember to turn the flip sign from "Closed" to "Open." The really sad thing? I couldn't always figure out if I forgot to turn it, or turned it twice. The really interesting thing? When you are the one in the shop, the rest of the world is "Closed" to you. Flip it when you are leaving, the rest of the world is "Open."

Nothing like getting a retailer's notification saying that, "Next weekend's rodeo will NOT be canceled as a result of the local outbreak of Horse Herpes." Uh, okay. Yippeee Kayay?!

I am commonly told that I think too much, so imagine my delight when a lady in the bookstore said she'd love to spend some time in my head because, "I think it would be fascinating." I felt complimented and was pleased, right up until she was getting ready to leave and said, "Forget that head time, that would be too much 'Flowers for Algernon' for me." Full marks for the self-deprecating version of, "You think too much."

On first take, you might conclude that there really is a cosmic appreciation for the ridiculous. How else might one explain that a couple, with numerous people to choose from, asked me, someone who's never had a driver's license, for directions to the DMV? But on second glance, you might surmise that I have extensive navigating experience, which would mean a cosmic appreciation for the sublime. Here's to steering them the right way.

I had someone call me one day at the bookstore to ask if I sold scrolls. "Uh, no. Yes, mine are used books, but more of the bound variety." (And that's with me forgoing calling my place Lord's Books. Imagine if I'd called the place "R Lord's Books." I'da had people asking for stone tablets.)

I love instant karma! When the theatre wasn't open during the day I accepted their packages for them. One day, I made a total hash of my signature when signing for them. (The expression you just got, how does someone make a hash of their own signature? Yeah, same one delivery guy had.) So the next day I said, "I'll maybe even get my signature on there right this time." To which delivery guy said, with an obvious inner laugh, "Like riding a bike, you'll get it back. It's all about remembering what to do." Well, off he headed to leave a notice for the theater but was distracted by someone stopping him and forgot to leave the notice. He soooo heard about that the next time I saw him. "Can I get you some training wheels for that bike of yours?"

For all those people who say you can tell a lot about a person by the books on their shelves: "Yes, I understand that you are looking for a yoga book but as I explained, I only carry leisure reading. Yes, I get that you consider yoga books leisure reading because you only leaf through them and never actually try the work-outs, but that doesn't change the fact that I don't have any." Guessing she wasn't doing the Happy Baby Pose after talking to me and realizing I wasn't going to be able to help people see from her bookshelf that she was bringing her mind and body together via the ancient practice. More likely she was trying out a new pose–like maybe the Downward Hang-dog.

If you've ever wondered what a reverse book snob looks like, look no further. No, I didn't have a devoted "classics" section in my bookstore. They were written for the masses at the time of publication, just like all the other "trash" in my shop. But by all means, feel free to try to "school" me on the error of my thinking. However, probably best to gear up for some serious trash talk if you're going to go there. (Just my little heads-up for those folks out there who'd come into my place spewing garbage.)

I dislike gritty, grimy books and as we live in the desert, and lots of folks stored their books in garages or sheds, yes, I washed the trade-in books at the bookstore. Of course, I didn't wash the ones I wasn't keeping because it was soooo much easier to get folks to take them off my hands when I'd tell them they were dirty books.

Me, a klutz, just because I manage to trip over sidewalks all the time? Nah! I'm going with the Sheriff's take, instead. I was walking home (fast–it was a Friday.) and I got distracted by the Main Street bat (he showed up every summer and just hung around downtown), hit the uneven sidewalk, and the laws of physics kicked in. Sheriff (after I came to a halt within a few feet of him), "Five giant steps and a no-hand save from a facer. Impressive! Thought I was going to be digging sidewalk scum out of your face but no, you got skills." (Hard-earned, to be sure.) And Wii called me unbalanced. Scoff.

Yes, indeed, I spent many a day on Main Street telling people where to go, where to get off at. And then there were days when it was a tourist and I was giving them directions.

Who could have guessed my A-frame sidewalk sign was multi-purpose? It was advertising for me, but also a great place to park it for some shade when you are a tiny tot and tired of the adult persons yakking away about nothing that interests you. So cute!

The things you learn about people when they go from being customers to friends. I've had a friend for many years (who shall not remain nameless: Jenifer) that I met in the early days of the bookstore. However, I would not have guessed, from the first visit, that we'd ever be friends, seeing as how she and her husband were going out of their way to stay as far away from me as they could get. When they walked in the door I told them my standard, "If there's anything I can help you with, just let me know," which was followed by the woman starting to speak, movement into one of the aisles, some hushed exchanges, and then the man telling me what he was looking for. When I got up to go over and help him find the books, they were both kind of backing away, then her husband hustled off down a different aisle and she took over listing the books. A little strange, but not wholly remarkable until they were getting ready to leave and the husband handed the wife his wallet to pay for the books, rather than come up to the desk himself. I had no idea what that was all about (sniffing my pits later having assured me that wasn't it), until months later, when we became friends, and I learned that her husband was having a gas problem for which she had been, in hushed tones, telling him to get away from her so I wouldn't think it was her and then telling him to stay away from me so he didn't gas the nice bookstore lady.

Just when you think e-books are going to make your shop defunct, a new business plan walks in the door and presents itself: cut "stash holes" in the middle of my books. I had a lady in the shop who was systematically working her way through my books, opening each one and then re-shelving it until she finally worked up the nerve to ask me where a pot shop was. (My guess? She had just obtained a medical card and thought my "Get Lit" t-shirts meant I'd know.) I had to ask her, "Did you think I was one and hiding my 'real' inventory in the books? And if so, why didn't you start with something like 'The Secret Garden?'"

It's all fun and games until someone shows their fangs. I had a guy come in on October 31st and go right to the Anne Rice books. He told me he started reading her after he was homeless in Denver and living under a bridge. He said a vampire flew down from the bridge, ripped the throat out of one guy, and then attacked him. He said he fought the vampire off, but not before he took a bite out of him. He then proceeded to pull his shirt down to show me the puncture wounds. How happy was I that it was a cold Halloween and I was wearing a turtle neck?! Yikes!

I had a little contretemps with a downtown neighbor one day (there were days when it was all rainbows and unicorns on Main Street and there were days when it was not) that caused me to go right past getting my city up (how Marty describes it when I get sarcastically irate) and right into getting my military (brat) up. That's "Bring it!" mode, most easily identified by my "Go to hell" soundtrack: Nazareth, Judas Priest, Black Sabbath and the like. I had told that to the FedEx guy and so when he came in and heard what I was playing, he put his hands up and said, "I come in peace, bearing gifts to R Lord." The next day I was asked about it by twenty-somethings from a neighboring business who had heard about it and I told them, "I've been fired from volunteer jobs for getting into people's faces over what I consider fundamentally wrong and I have walked away from jobs because of things that other people considered minor and no, I won't be yanking that 'uptight' stick out of my ass, now." Young person, "You did not say that!" Yeah, I did. There's a reason I was a sole proprietor.

Yep, I have skills. A gentleman came into the shop and I started speaking to him at "shop volume" and he said, "Dammit, I forgot my hearing aids! No way I'm going to be able to hear you," so I started speaking to him at "Dad volume" (my Dad has been hard-of-hearing all my life), and he reached up to check if his hearing aids were in, after all. (There's just no escaping me when I mean to be heard.)

Tales of the reticent man. There was a man who walked his dog down Main Street pretty near every day one season. Though we'd crossed paths a number of times outdoors, he had never acknowledged a verbal greeting, a wave, or a smile from me. I didn't know why, but I still smiled, waved, said hello–and dubbed him, in my mind, the reticent man. Then one day we crossed paths when he was walking without his pupper so I said, "I hope your dog is well." He stopped and said, "The dog went after the chickens, so I shot him." I said, "No, you didn't. You love that dog." He then laughed, told me the dog was well, and we had a nice little chat. I then knew his name, the pupper's name, and some other miscellaneous details about his life. We parted company without me knowing if that was an aberration or if he'd acknowledge a smile, wave, or hello in the future and as it turned out, the next day brought an opportunity to find out. I waved at him when I saw him walking on the other side of the street and though he saw me, no, he didn't wave back. Rude! But not wholly unexpected. Then he crossed over to walk down my side of the street and I went to greet him and realized it wasn't him. (Really?! How many guys with a ball cap, headphones and a fishing rod could possibly be walking around downtown? Well, at least two.) A few days later I was pretty sure I saw him and his dog from across the street when I was meeting Marty at lunch and (phew!) knew for sure it was him as he yelled, "You were right, the dog is alive and well." We then crossed paths when I was walking back from lunch and he stopped to chat for a minute. That chat set the pattern for every future interaction. The reticent man would grumble about something like, "I have to go baby-sit the grandkids" and I'd say something to his dog like, "You're the one who really baby-sits, aren't you? He just takes the credit for it. Such a nice thing you do." And the dog would sagely nod. A few days later, "The weather is too cold to be walking. I don't know why I leave my warm house to take this old dog on walks." And I said to the dog, "Such a gentleman, taking your human for a walk, even in the cold." And he sagely nodded. Then one day we crossed paths when Marty was at the shop to pick me up. You kind of have to see this in action but, with the very rare exception, puppers adore Marty. On sight. Fall all over themselves, and him if they can, so it was no surprise to me when the dog glommed onto him. But then, so did the reticent man! He was so gregarious I asked Marty later if he smelled alcohol. Maybe weed? It then became a pattern for the reticent man to bring the dog by my shop and allow a few minutes to meet and greet. On one of those occasions I told him that the dog looked a little tired and he said, "I don't know why, all he did was sleep while I watched the grandkids." The dog's head whipped around and he looked at his human like, "Seriously?!" So I said to the dog, "It's okay, we all know you were the one doing the real work." And the dog scooched over, leaned on my leg, and smiled at his human. I didn't see them for a little while after that, not until I was walking back to the shop from lunch with a friend and saw the man, without his dog, and to my "Hello" he said, "The dog isn't dead." I laughed and said, "Oh, good! Say hi to him for me." And then we were fully past each other and the friend looked at me and said, "I so want to know but I'm not going to ask. Wouldn't want to ruin that moment with details." They became such a pleasant part of that season that I was truly saddened on the day I got a rap on my shop door and went out to find the pair, there to tell me that they were leaving town. I told the dog that I knew he'd take good care of his human and he sagely nodded, then departed with a smile and wag.

You just can't hide the Lordliness! There was an elementary-school-aged young lady that I came across every now and again downtown who thought I walked on water. (And didn't even know my last name!) I saw her one day and she was a little downcast when she told me she has to bring her lunches to school that year because her folks couldn't afford to buy them. I said, "That's one way to look at it." She asked, "What do you mean?" I said, "You get to bring your lunch to school. That means you get to help pick what you want to eat, you get to help make it, and you get to have a fruit-vegetable other than ketchup." She asked if I used to carry my lunch to school and I said, "Absolutely! Money was tight at my house, too. And really, does anyone other than yourself ever make a peanut-butter-and-jelly sandwich just right?" She decided if bringing a lunch to school was good enough for me, it was good enough for her, too. When her Dad told her it was time to go, she was describing her lunchbox to me, and all she'd be able to bring in it. There's peer pressure, and then there's peer of the realm.

The things that make being a shopkeeper on Main Street grand: I once had a lady come in my shop and she said, "I just need to talk to myself for a minute and if I do it on the street, people will think I'm nuts. Do you mind?" I didn't mind, and gave her leave to go ahead. However, the very small nature of my shop meant I did eavesdrop, and it was quite the conversation she had with herself, all about how to deal with a difficult coworker. She stopped by again a while later and said, "I don't need to talk to myself, I just wanted to say hello." Me, "That's too bad. I was all ready to take notes this time for dealing with that witch I work for."

A friend who is a master quilter taught me the basics of hand quilting in the early years of the bookstore as a means for me to be doing something in my small shop that folks felt comfortable interrupting me at. I wasn't great at it, as evidenced by the customer I had in the shop who spoke English as a second language. As if English isn't a hard enough language, add in idioms and how what you say is heard instead of what you meant, and you can end up having an entirely different conversation than you intended when you say, "reaping what I sowed" because their primary language reads an "i" as a long "e" and, they are agreeing with you that you do indeed need to be ripping what you sewed. So, I moved on to crochet (all sorts of irony in that for me since interrupting me while I'm reading is just not a problem for me, but made other people uncomfortable, whereas anything other than basic crochet patterns requires counting, so interrupting that would have been problematic, which is why I only ever learned basic stitches, and have only crocheted potholders, and giant potholders; otherwise known as blankets). My method of crochet is truly cringe-worthy for people accomplished at the skill. I don't hold everything the traditional way, and rather stab away at some yarn with a hook, so it's not a smooth or relaxing-looking activity when I'm doing it. I had more than one person wince and then say something along the lines of, "It's not a battle between you and the yarn. You don't have to wrestle it into submission." Me, "Maybe you don't...."

Yes, there were some days downtown when I really didn't have anything better to do than contemplate the ways of the world. Like, there are some businesses downtown that have living quarters upstairs but no, mine wasn't one of them. But really, how cool would it be to live above a bookstore? Even better, a hotel above a bookstore. It would bring all new meaning to room service, "I'll take A Catcher in the Rye with a side of Grapes of Wrath... Three Musketeers for dessert."

If I ever run into you and don't recognize you right away, really, don't take it personally. Marty came into the bookstore one day and I didn't immediately recognize him and I've known him since I was fifteen years old. Though in my own defense I will say that showing up looking like one of the Village People (wearing a hardhat and reflective vest–he's an estimator/project manager for heavy highway construction), does make "YMCA" go through your mind before anything else. (You know it's what went through yours the minute you heard Village People, too.)

I never quite got a grasp on why so many solicitors would work, "Nice Christian woman like you" somewhere into their spiel. And they certainly weren't expecting me to respond with, "That's two out of three assumptions made in the absence of any evidence to support your conclusion." The moment of silence while they were processing that one? An answer to a prayer.

I love when young people put their creativity to use and try out new and different things. Which explains why, when I ran into one of my favorite young downtown employees and he asked if I'd like to try a new drink he created, I agreed. It also explains why I just suggested he call it a mimosa, rather than tell him that was already its name. (He thought it a perfect name. And why wouldn't he?!)

If I ever travel to the Netherlands, I'm making sure I have lots of change on me for parking. (Or not, since I don't drive. And because they probably only take cards, these days. But that's just details.) I had a gentleman come into the shop to ask about how to pay for parking. His English was limited, and my Dutch non-existent. I told him it was free, and he asked me where the meter was. I told him it was free, and he asked me where the booth was. I told him it was free, and he asked me where the cart (?) was. He having apparently exhausted his repertoire of English words on how to ask about parking, I tried to explain that while we have timed limits on daytime parking, he was outside of those hours, so he was good to go. That worked so well he then went back outside and stood by the car while his family left to go gad-about. Thinkin' since "free parking" was just not a concept he was familiar with, I went out and offered to watch the car from the shop for him so he could join his family; which is how I learned that a shooing motion, accompanied by me saying, "Go, go," is apparently universal.

I was trying to tell Marty how to do something he already knew how to do one day and he said, "Really?!" Me, "Well, now you know what it's like for me, putting up with that witch I work for."

I was such a downtown instigator, even when I wasn't trying to be. On "May the Fourth be with you" I was telling the FedEx guy, a big Star Wars fan, about some deal I had read with regard to Han Solo saying, about the Millennium Falcon, "It's the ship that made the Kessel Run in less than twelve parsecs." Seems a bunch of geeks were arguing that since parsecs describe length, and not time, he was misusing the word "parsec." But then a bunch of uber-geeks came in to explain how, by skirting black holes and such, he could have shortened the length. FedEx guy told me the next day that he had a stop at a business where the owner, and some employees, were huge Star Wars fans and he started a big debate on that issue there. When he left, they were growling at each other like Wookiees, "Wyaaaaaa! Vlarrrr muurrrgh rrgggg lurrrr. Brrr-annn gooowwrrrgh. Grrooooogrrraaaawrrrrrrrrmph. Grrrrrrrrgaahga." (Apologies for my really bad accent but you get the drift, I'm sure.)

My Mom always told us daughters, "It's not what I say, it's how you hear it." And, having been raised with a severely hard-of-hearing parent (my Dad, who required clear speech), I certainly wasn't going to argue the point, even if that's not quite the context she was addressing. Then I got a whole new demonstration of the versatility of that concept when I got a misdirected package and called UPS to tell them. Their automated voice thingy told me it didn't understand me and asked me to repeat myself: three times. Then it switched to Spanish. I'm tellin' ya, the struggle is real when enunciating is heard as a whole other language.

I was actually raised right when it comes to answering the phone. I originally answered the bookstore phone by saying, "Punchak's Paperbacks, this is Roxanne, how may I help you?" But, telemarketers caused me to do away with that. They'd call using my name, like they knew me. So, I amused myself for a while by answering the phone, "Punchak's Paperbacks, this is Me, how may I help you?" ("How do you spell that?" Me, "M-e.") Then I'd know it was a telemarketer on a repeat call because they'd ask for "Me." "Is Me available?" Me, "I don't know, are you?"

You can't really call yourself a downtown business without someone trying to con you out of something. Man, "I'm here selling grass-fed beef, if you're interested." Me, "Where are you from?" Man, "Colorado Springs." Me, "And you came to farm and ranch country to sell beef, why?" Man, "Ours is better." Me, "How's that?" Man, "It doesn't eat sage like the beef does here." Me, "And you know that because what, it only eats your lawn?" Man, "Okaaay. I have seafood, too. Not farmed, fresh." Me, "From the ocean in your backyard?" I thought I was waaaay funnier than he did... he backed out of there so fast you'd have thought I was trying to sell him something.

Life in the small-town small-business lane: I had a guy Marty used to work with stop by our house, looking for books, because he was rained out from work, needed a book, and I was closed on Mondays. I felt sorry for him (I know what it's like to jones for reading material) so gave him a few out of my "to read" stash, but warned him that I wouldn't do that again. Guy, "No problem, next time I'll just pick you up and drive you up there so I can go through the shelves." (Well, huh. Not quite where I was going with that.) I got another visit from him after I permanently closed the bookstore, "The bookstore is closed?! For good? It can't be closed, I need books! You must have a garage full of books here." (I did not. I donated my books to AmVets and Friends of the Library when I closed; however, I did manage to find a few for him–and then gave him directions to the other used bookstore.)

Our theater is only open for matinees when the kids are not in school, so the rest of the year I would accept daily packages on their behalf. One day, I ran into the FedEx guy on the street, who I was no longer seeing because the theatre was open during delivery hours, and I subjected him to (think Barbra Streisand and Neil Diamond): "You don't bring me posters, you don't bring me movies. You don't want me to sign anymore, for packages galore, in the midst of the day." Being the nice man he is, he brought me a candy bar the next day.

I had a lot of great discussions and debates at the bookstore over the years, and it always fascinated me, the need some folks have to crowd your personal space when involved in one. I have to say I was partial to their facial expression when I'd say, "You know, towering over me doesn't make you right, it just makes you taller. Hardly a notable feat seeing as how I'm just shy of five-foot-two." If that didn't work, I'd hand them a breath mint, from the cache I kept on hand just for that purpose. Guaranteed to make someone back up.

I had a gentleman who patronized the bookstore regularly who wore suspenders with a measuring-tape pattern. He came in on what would normally have been a work day for him and let me know that he had just dropped a dead mountain lion off to the taxidermist. He told me the mountain lion had evidently been up on his telephone pole, hit the wrong wires, shocked itself to death, and landed in his truck bed, where the gentleman found him when he got up for work that morning. So, his boss gave him a paid "Really?!" day. Me, "How big was it?" Gentleman, "Big, but I don't know, exactly." Me, "You didn't take off your suspenders and measure it?!" Some people!

A couple of years after I opened the bookstore I had a lady try to trade in a romance novel wherein a glance inside (I always flipped through the books) showed that it looked like an FBI dossier. When asked, she told me she had "redacted" every swear word and every racy scene. And then when I told her, no, I wouldn't take a permanent-markered-up book in trade, she acted all affronted; like keeping all the good stuff to herself was a public service or something. (She had to read it to redact it, after all.)

You know you are in a small town when: The shopkeeper tells you they'll be back in a minute, feel free to just browse around in the meantime. (What can you do? I didn't have a restroom in the shop, had to run upstairs, and some things just can't wait.) You know you have been reminded of the fundamental goodness of people when: In 23 years I never had one person leave the shop while I was gone. Even if they didn't buy anything, they stayed to watch it for me, even though I hadn't requested that. How cool is that?

When you walk to work, you can run into a number of things that delay you, even when you've built in plenty of time. (Including the road rising up to meet you. Just with me, that was more a literal thing than an Irish blessing, and I have the scars on my hands to prove it.) I was late one day because I had veered a bit off course to help someone in a wheelchair go up a hill and when I arrived, I had to deal with an annoyed city person who didn't get the slower pace of small towns. Since they made a point of pointing out that my hours sign said 11:00 and it was not 11:00 when I arrived, I changed my hours sign to "11:00-

ish until closing." It was rather a snark on my part but tourists loved it so much that even that witch I worked for had to admit it was a good call, and stopped threatening to dock my pay whenever I was late.

Had to love my neighbors' expression when they came by to vent that the internet was down so they couldn't finish their work and I said, "Really? Because it's working just fine here and since I pirate yours…" Gotta love it even more when you're having a problem getting online and since you are pirating theirs, you ask them to come take a look but really, why wouldn't you? I know a lot of people see young people with their full focus on electronics and think all sorts of negative things, but me? I saw troubleshooters just looking for a problem to solve.

Just my luck that on one of those days when it seemed like everything that could go wrong, did, I couldn't even claim sleep deprivation as the cause, seeing as how the very long, very deep, pillow crease in my left cheek would have put the lie to that statement before I even finished uttering it. It started at the post office on my way to work. I dropped a penny, bent to pick it up, realized my shoe was untied, went to tie it, my hat fell off, then when I started to stand, my wallet fell out of my purse. I had to say to the man who not so kindly remarked on it, "Why yes, I am a walking disaster area this morning. So it'd probably be better if you just back up a few feet before I 'accidentally' drop you on the ground." And the rest of the day went downhill from there. You ever notice how sleep-crease days always end up being a nightmare? It's an omen, I tell you!

The little regional things you never even think of until interacting with tourists. I walked by a pupper sitting in the driver's seat of a street buggy, waiting for his person. When his person passed me he was carrying two drink containers. I commented on how nice it was of him to get a pop for his chauffeur, too. He didn't know what a pop was. We

47

then managed a whole conversation on pop, soda and soda pop; not nearly as interesting to the dog, since what he was getting was water, no ice.

When North meets South. Don't ever let anyone tell you about all those fine Southern manners because I know, from first-hand experience, they aren't always all that fine. Like, no matter how often you interrupt a Southerner to get them back on track they will doggedly, and rudely, continue till they reach the end of a paragraph. Uh, I mean, sentence. Seriously, do we not consider it the polite thing to redirect someone who is, say, walking into a quagmire? How is talking any different? That was the kind of teasing that would go on between me and the FedEx guy from the South. Then he came into the shop one day when my folks were there and I introduced them and said, "You're from Mississippi, right?" FedEx guy, "Yes, I'm from the capital of Mississippi: Memphis, Tennessee. Northerners! You talk so fast you lose your way."

Oh yeah, I'm a sentimental sap. One of the great things about a downtown business is a reserved spot at every parade. You'd hear the marching band and know you were in for a good show. One of my favorites was when a diverse family (E Pluribus Unum) parked in front of my shop and then sat in the back of their pick-up truck. When the flags at the front of the processional approached the parents stood and said to the kids, who were still seated, "Stand up for the American Flag, what it represents is important." Each kid grabbed a hand and stood. Nice moment.

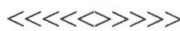

You know, I've often thought that every year we should rotate the work-week by one day: Mon-Fri, Tues-Sat, Wed-Sun, etc. so that poor Monday isn't always sitting on its own as the most hated day of the week. (Long holiday weekends don't count, 'cause folks don't really love Monday, they love the holiday from Monday.) Because really, how would you feel if every time most folks saw you coming they started complaining? How many times have you heard someone say, "Thank God it's Monday!"? Opening my shop just confirmed me in that thought because even though I worked Tuesday-Saturday, that just made Tuesday into Monday–and I can prove it. If Tuesday is always Tuesday, I would not have put my sidewalk sign with the arrow on it facing the street, rather than the shop, one morning. But since in my case Tuesday was Monday, even though it was Tuesday, I did. That's because when Monday is Tuesday, then Tuesday is Monday, and so Monday is nice to you but Tuesday is not–and pulls little pranks on you like that one. (And if you managed to follow all of that, today is definitely not your Monday.)

Over the course of my tenure as a Main Street shop there were a number of different tenants in the building next door. At one time it was even a mini-police station, which I was rather excited about until I realized they weren't putting in a mini-jail and giving me a new customer base for my books. Nevertheless, the Cortez Police Department Community Resource Center ended up being very entertaining for me: from looking at the little kids coming out after having been fingerprinted for their ID kits and thinking that some of them were going to be back later in life (just not nearly as excited about the whole process) to my discussions with the Police Chief about community policing. I honestly didn't get the concept of a community cop shop where the officers didn't wander around downtown and introduce themselves to everybody (I mean really, they were the first neighbors I ever had who didn't come by to chat about what was going on in town and I thought we were paying them to be nosy?), so I decided to talk to the Police Chief about it. However, that was a bust (minus the handcuffs, thank goodness) and I therefore determined that if they weren't going to come around and get the latest on-dit (even if they had their reasons) that it was my civic duty to go next door and introduce myself to the rotating officers and grill them about what they were doing. One day the officer I was introducing myself to said, "So, you just moved in next door?" To which I responded, "No, you did. I've been here over fourteen years, but thanks for so succinctly making my point." Then I got exactly what I had not exactly been asking for when the cops started paying attention to what I was doing and thus questioned my common sense. (And there I was thinking that it had already been well established that I don't have much. Huh.) Uh-huh. Make friends with the cops next door and the next thing you know they are chiding you for having left your door unlocked when you went upstairs to the restroom. I had to retaliate by saying, "You know, leaving an idling police car at the curb is like a waving a big old 'Joyride' flag, even to a non-driver like me." I met many of the local cops during that time, all hard-working and committed individuals. So definitely do take a minute to thank a cop during National Police Week, even if it's the Police Chief and, much to his dismay, you managed to corner him in the cop shop before he had a chance to get away. (Kidding! He was always civil.)

"As far as I can see" is an incredibly common phrase here. I hear it often. But, it does take on a slightly different character when uttered by a sightless person. I passed a blind gentleman who was coming out of the post office on my way to work and I said, "Good morning." He said, "Good morning to you. And how are you today?" I said, "Great! How about yourself?" He said, "Doing fine," then gifted me with a wicked smile and said, "As far as I can see, anyway."

When my folks parked on the end of the street that caused them to pass my shop on their way to lunch they generally stopped in to say hello, and then they'd wave at me on their way back by. I missed the wave one day, but saw them right before they were out of view of my door so went out to wish them a good afternoon. Got to the sidewalk and never ended up speaking. I watched my folks, from behind, walking to the end of the block. My Dad holding my Mom's arm, steadying her. My Mom leaning into my Dad. Their movements not at all smooth (my Mom had young-onset Parkinson's disease) and yet, so smoothly aligned with each other. Beauty in emotion. How fortunate was I, to have been granted such a view? A mind-picture that fills the heart.

I am a re-user so bottled water for me tends to mean water in a repurposed glass bottle with a screw-on lid. That raises no eyebrows at all when it's an old pop bottle but raised all sorts of them when it was a maple syrup bottle; which is why I would use one, on occasion. It was fun to watch those brows raise, then beetle, as folks tried to figure out what they were looking at. And then to see their eyes light up with amusement when they asked, "Is that a syrup bottle?!" And then one day, "What do you have in there? Because that sure looks like a flask." Well huh, hadn't thought of that…

"Hopscotch to it!" Those were the words written under the course chalked out in front of a business I passed one day when I was a teen. And, I did. Without falling, even, so I didn't have to act like, "What? I'm not a klutz, that's just a move I learned playing Twister as a kid." I enjoyed that so much that one of my favorite days downtown, ever, was in the early years of the bookstore when I got the theatre kids together and we chalked a hopscotch board on our shared sidewalk to recreate the experience. Almost no one could resist, and we watched people hop their way toward a movie all day. Sadly, never to be repeated because of liability issues. But, it was one great day!

I'm not much of one for traditional small talk so for a change of pace one day, I challenged myself to talk about absolutely nothing but the weather with every person I ran into downtown. Conversational gambits went along the lines of: "It only took me one–count it, one–day of freezing my butt off on the walk to and from work to realize that I needed to hunt down my heavier jacket. Look at me go! The Neanderthal's would be so proud!" and, "I smiled all the way on my walk to work today, seeing as how I knew my face was going to freeze into whatever expression I had on it," or, "Yeah, I know I'm all bundled up. But, there's so much snow that I could only conclude that since rain hadn't managed to melt that witch I work for, Mother Nature brought out the big guns: water that would stick to hard-to-melt witches. Just to be safe, I had to don a hazmat suit–otherwise known as snow clothes–in case she mistook me for that witch, seeing as how we look so much alike," or, "Whew! People are so blown away by what they are seeing in my display window that the wind they are generating is ringing my bell with phantom customers and knocking over my sidewalk sign." (My door opened inward, so wind would make my bell ring.) Topic of conversation downtown the next day? "Possession, alien abduction, drugs, or some other unseen menace and how it has affected the bookstore lady."

I don't generally want to just know how I should do something, I also want to know why I can't do it a different way, so a conversation with my Dad (a retired CPA) about my shop bookwork:
Me, "What if I do it this way?"
My Dad, "This will happen."
Me, "What if I do it that way?"
My Dad, "That will happen."
Me, "This is purely academic but what if do it this'a, that'a way?"
My Dad, (throwing up his hands), "Great idea! You can this'a, that'a all day long if you can convince twelve other people–who will be sitting in a box together–to see it your way."

I signed "R Lord" for all the packages I received at my shop, which caused the FedEx guy to say, when I had one delivered there that I told him was for Marty's birthday, which is Christmas Day, "Oh my God, R Lord and Jesus Lord? Is there a star on your house?!" I said, "Marty's last name isn't Lord, it's Punchak." He said, "Oh, I always wondered how you got the name for the bookstore." (It was Punchak's Paperbacks.) I said, "Hard to believe, I know, that it wasn't because I realized that 'Lord's Books' would be a bit confusing, seeing as how it wasn't a Christian bookstore, so I decided to go rhyming alliterative instead and went looking for some obscure Ukrainian? Polish? Who the hell actually knows? name, found that one and went, 'That's the one to put on my shop!' but, that's not what actually happened." Then I wished him a Happy Martinmas since that's what I call Dec 25th, the day a great man was born unto my world.

The most debated sign on my shop door? The one I'd put up saying, "Back in two minutes" for when I'd head upstairs to the restroom. Folks had all sorts of opinions about whether or not two minutes was a proper number to pick (why? Beats me. But it definitely seemed to matter to some folks), none of which swayed me. I used the same time for twenty-three years. Yes, it's short (and therefore more likely to keep people from walking away) and yes, I can use a restroom and wash and dry my hands in short order not only because I was raised in a household with eight people (seven of them women) and one bathroom, but because I'm also of the generation who ran for it during TV commercial breaks which were, yes, usually two-minute breaks. And yes, I called dibs on my seat before I left so that the witch I worked for wouldn't steal it while I was gone.

The UPS driver with the downtown route was a really nice man but not a talker or much given to smiling. He was on the clock and on the move when we saw him, so it was usually just a quick wave. Thus, it was quite the moment to see his big grin after the theatre manager flagged him down, rather than waiting for him to come at his normal time, because they were expecting an item they desperately needed for a repair. They rather urgently said, "You should have something for me in there." UPS guy said yes and went to the back of the van to get it. He then handed over a poster and said, "Not sure what all the fuss is about for a poster, but here you go." Theatre manager, "Oh no! That's not what I needed!" and UPS guy said, "Oh, sorry. Maybe this will make you feel better" and then reached behind himself and pulled out the box with the part in it." Psych! No one does it better than the more serious-natured.

Had a brave man in the bookstore one day. He directed his young kids (maybe four and six) to his favorite genre and then let them pick out his books for him. At first I was thinking how cute it was, watching them looking at covers to get just the right books for Dad. Then I really paid attention to where they were picking from and realized that if I could get more parents to do that, I could totally start selling the books off the lower shelves. Brilliant!

A perfectly good plan, ruined! I should have looked it up online but instead I asked Marty how to forward calls and he started telling me and then got a suspicious look on his face and wanted to know why I wanted to know, so I had to tell him that since the vast majority of calls to my shop were outsourced sales calls, I thought the perfect solution to the problem would be to make him my outsourced "No!" person. And it sorta worked: he said, very convincingly, "No!"

Because it's not enough that small businesses are captive audiences to anyone who walked through our doors, we'd get random stuff in the mail, too. I got a letter addressed to "Punchak's"—no return address, no salutation, no signature, from some random guy who wanted me to know that he moved to his current city in '94, is a Christian who knows God, was released from prison in 2004, was on parole, enrolled in an alcohol program, and hooked up with an older woman. And that was just the lead-in to a three-page rambling dissertation on the "New World Order" and how "Intelligent Transportation Systems" are being used to institute it, and the last days that are coming. All that so that he could complain to me about having to ride the bus because of gas prices. And there I was, reading his letter from a town that doesn't have any buses so there was no way he could walk through my door and express his complaints in person. Darn!

I was so showin'-n-tellin' my old Pee-Chee to the teenagers downtown after I learned that (horrors) they'd never seen one in real life. But only, of course, after I asked if they could guess how many times I had detention and which Breakfast Club detainee I might have been. (Ask someone that, sometime. So fun to hear the answers!)

I bought my first laptop for use in the bookstore. Young theatre folks noticed that I still had the plastic piece that covered the dead areas on the keyboard and then laughed themselves silly when I told them that was because it's a crumb-catcher for when I'm snacking. (Don't even. Lift it up, wipe it off, how is that a bad plan?!) Then I told them about how I spilled a glass of water on the keyboard and, lo and behold, the crumb-catcher saved my device. Uh-huh. Just got your attention, didn't I? How much you wanna bet they now keep their crumb-catchers, too?

I would go by the theatre to buy candy solely as a means of introducing myself to new employees (that's my story, sticking to it) but I hadn't yet been by to buy when I saw a new theatre kid out washing the windows with the hose, enjoying playing with the water. I asked if he'd be drying my window off, now that he got it all wet. He looked around, realized he didn't have anything to dry the windows with (because they didn't actually dry the windows after a hose washing. Yes, I'm just that kind of irksome) and after I smiled and explained to him that they dry well as long as they are clean and well-rinsed, he offered to do my window as well so they'd dry nicely, too. I thanked him, said I'd appreciate it. Then I introduced myself and he said, "Yeah, you're the lady who gets the Reese's and chocolate-covered almonds." See! It worked so well, I didn't even have to actually buy the candy to get the result. (Oh wait, that last sentence came out wrong. Backspace, backspace, backspace. Forget I ever said that.)

You see lots of motorhomes in a town surrounded by state and national parks so I suppose it was inevitable that I would one day see the Joneses driving down the street in the biggest motorhome with the biggest attached motorhome garage I'd ever seen. And right behind them, the Smiths trying to keep up in an identical rig, apparently jumping in so fast in order to not be left behind, their side door was open and flapping back and forth. And then there was me, not quite fleet of foot enough to keep up with either one. But hey, my yelling and waving did make a motorhome a few cars behind them pull over and check their rig to make sure all was in place, so there was that.

It's true that it often takes people in small towns a while to view newcomers as locals. And, there aren't many ways around that. One way that definitely isn't going to work is to answer my question, "Where are you visiting us from?" by saying, "Oh, I'm a local. I'm from Mancos" but by pronouncing the town's name the proper Spanish way, and not the improper local way. Me, "And when you've been here a little while longer, you'll be from Mancos." Lady, "Gave myself away, did I?" Mmmm-hmmm.

I never would have guessed, when I opened the bookstore, that one of the things I'd become well-versed in was the number of pages in classic novels, but I undeniably did. High school student (one of many), "I need a book for a book report." Me, "What are your interests?" Student, "Oh, I don't care what it's about, it just has to be a minimum of one-hundred-and-ninety pages and as few over that as possible." Me, "But if it's interesting, the page numbers shouldn't matter." High school student, "Tell that to my teacher, who said my paper has to be no less than two pages and no more than five." Touché!

I officially closed the bookstore on 11/11/11 and then I spent the Thanksgiving weekend after boxing up the books for donation. I didn't have to be there on Thursday because even that witch I worked for wasn't a big enough turkey to do that to me but still, it was a hard weekend. After boxing up some fifteen hundred high-shelved books (up the ladder, down the ladder) I even tried starting a fight with myself so I could stomp off in a snit and not have to finish but, huh, it was all still there when I came back.

Once it was clear that I was closing the bookstore at least one person a day stopped by to ask if they could have my bookcases. I'd ask, "What would be your plan for getting them out of here?" (We built them floor-to-ceiling on site. They were never going out the door as bookcases.) No one had a good one so, yeah, I had to take them all down to lumber when I switched the shop from a bookstore to a tourist shop. I was feeling all sorts of brilliant when I figured out (after a couple three) that it is sooo much easier to remove shelves if you take the shelf off the brackets before removing them from the wall; and then I ran into a bracket with my forehead. The bookshelf version of a head-flick, apparently, to remind me that I was not yet smarter than the shelves. Once I got them all down, I swear, I had thousands of screws of every type ever made. They made me figure that if all else failed with my new business venture I could totally open a screw store; until I realized there'd be something fundamentally wrong with a shop named, "Roxanne's Top-of-the-Line to Discount Screws." That'd just be begging The Police to conduct a Sting operation. (Admit it, that was a top-shelf groaner, for sure!)

When I get tired, I get silly (and now I know why it's called a punch list... 'cause you get seriously punch drunk after too much time focused on it) and after boxing thousands of books after I closed the bookstore I was definitely tired, but I swear I heard all those characters in those books jabbering away at each other, trying to figure out what was going on. The worst was when I closed the tops of the boxes and they all went, "Heyyyyyy, it's dark in here!" I promised them light at the end of their journey.

How truly great was Punchak's Paperbacks? So great that years after I closed it, it was still being entered (not by me.) in the annual "The Best of Montezuma County" (Restaurants, Auto Repair, etc.) contest. Won honorable mentions, even. It was so exceptional that American Express offered Punchak's Paperbacks a hefty limit on a credit card–four years after it closed. All that raised my expectations so high that the next year I was lamenting, "They forget so soon! Only five years since I closed Punchak's Paperbacks and this year it wasn't in the contest in the bookstore category for 'Best of Cortez and Montezuma County.' Bummer!" On the plus side, it also meant that someone finally noticed it wasn't a bookstore anymore. Which meant it was moving from being "The bookstore you go by" (when giving someone directions) to "Where the bookstore used to be." Took a little while longer for it to become "Where the tourist shop is." Small towns, don'tcha know?

You gotta give it up to that witch I used to work for, she was totally prescient! Yep, opened a bookstore on National Read a Book Day before it was National Read a Book Day. (September 6th.) She was Book Learned. Generous, too! After she closed Punchak's Paperbacks, but on the anniversary of opening it, she always made a general announcement: Free Books for Everyone! Available now at your local library.

It didn't really bode well for one company's shot at the contract for my replacement shop flooring when Marty's response to their bid number was, "I could pave the thing for less than that!" And Marty did end up doing the flooring for me, but vinyl plank, not asphalt, seeing as how it wasn't "Kokopelli's Getaways in the Asphalt Jungle." Though now that I think about it, that could have been a thing. (Kokopelli and Happy in the city, not the asphalt floor. Small businesses already deal with enough metaphorical potholes, don't need any real ones.)

I am entirely an "If it's not broken don't fix it, if it still works use it" kind of person. So for me, it was a big deal to finally let loose of the old college computer desk we hauled from Washington that I used as the desk for the bookstore all those years. (Not entirely gone from the shop, I just took off the hutch and it became the heat-press table.) Not sentimentally difficult as, truth be told, I never liked that old desk anyway, which is why it so totally cracked me up that someone who heard somewhere along the small-town way that I was going to be replacing that desk sent me an e-mail with an attached photo: offering to sell me an identical one. (I opened that attachment and went, "Hell to the no!") I politely demurred in favor of the beautiful one Marty built, that already did have sentimental value.

Marty and I are both short people, which is something we really don't think about much until a tall person comes to our house and we realize that our wall art hanging at the recommended "eye level" or our spare bathroom mirror hung to frame our faces (but hitting them at chest level), makes our house look like a hobbit house to them. So, good thing I looked up the average height of retail display shelves before we started sawing, 'cause the height we were getting ready to eyeball settle on was about four inches shy of the industry standard. Saved me from having to make up a story about we went with Ancient Puebloan average heights (which we are) for authenticity. You'd have bought that, right?

I closed the bookstore in the winter but didn't reopen as a tourist shop until the next spring, so warm weather finally came while we were re-purposing the wood from the bookstore to the tourist shop but, because of it, Marty turned blue. No, not sad: blue. Like a Smurf blue. He was working with the wood outdoors and the combination of lotion, sweat and wiping his hands on his new jeans–then wiping his hands on his head, face, neck–turned him blue. I wasn't sure I was seeing him right so I asked him to step back so I could see him in different light and he said, "What? You don't like blue bayou?" Ha!

There's a "right" tool for the job? Pshaw! The fixtures we built for the tourist shop were certainly a conversation starter as folks often remarked on the finished products. Most were complimentary, a few were critical, but none ever mistook them for mass-produced because we aren't folks who follow directions much. We tend to look at the materials at hand and try to find a way to make them work for what we want. (Because I'm a frugal minimalist. Marty? Not as much.) One day I had a young man say he wished he could build stuff like it but he didn't have the right tools. Me, "Neither does Marty. You are looking at a jig saw, sander, drill and hammer." Young guy, "Really?! I could get my hands on those." Such a moment for Marty when I told him, "See, you thought it might be nice to have 'proper' tools every now and again but if you did, you'd never have inspired a young guy to give it a go with improper ones." A head-shaking, eye-rolling moment, but still, a moment.

I really do so enjoy people. When I was changing over my shop I made an appointment with a local printer. He asked what it was pertaining to and I said, "I'm hoping to employ your skills but I also like to learn about processes so I'm looking to do printing for dummies, where I ask you all sorts of stupid questions, and you answer. Rolling your eyes is optional." He thought about it for a minute then said, "Okay, I can do that." And, he did–throwing in an eye roll just so I wouldn't feel cheated. (That was his story, anyway.)

My back wall at the shop was painted wood paneling that had been there for, well, forever. If appearances can be trusted, every tenant had hung and then removed things from that wall, and every tenant just threw up a glob of Spackle to cover the hole. I have no idea how many times the wall had been painted, but it appeared that no painter has ever felt moved to sand out the globs. I think they felt like they'd be messing with history or something since we certainly did, and so when we went and threw up our own globs, we didn't sand them, either. It was fun, to have contributed our little bit to the glob history–and to see people wrinkle their foreheads while trying try to decide if the wood came that way and it was a deliberate design choice.

A few months after my Mom died, my Dad upgraded his e-reader and gave me his old one. (Yes, I owned a bookstore and used an e-reader. Sue me.) When I went to read a book on it, I noticed there was a little metal ring on the magnetic strip that holds the book closed. I asked him what it was for and he said he'd never noticed it, and that it didn't come with the book. I then realized it had to have come from my Mom. When I was working on the keychains for my shop, the people I bought the metal rings from kindly sent me a bunch of different-sized rings and fittings so I could figure out what would work best. My Mom did all the experimenting for that for me, and must have been playing around with them when my Dad stuck his open book on the table where it picked one up with the magnetic closer, and no one noticed until I did when I got the book. A good luck charm, to be sure, that has moved to each new cover.

I was a bit brain-scattered when trying to get things done for the shop changeover and so I finally made a list detailing who was doing what, and how much and when I was going to owe. I included Marty and his projects, but left the rest blank for him. When I picked it up later to go over it, I found that he had filled in the payment part with, "Works for hugs... payment on demand." (Awwww!)

I was thrilled when Marty agreed to do the drawings for my switch to the tourist shop. He was reluctant at first, said, "I'm an engineer, not an artist." But I managed to convince him. And then I was like a kid on Christmas Eve waiting for Marty to e-mail updated pictures of the latest drawing he was perfecting while at wor... uh, I mean, lunch. Because me? I can't draw, not anything. Even my stick people look oddly out of proportion. But, for some unknown reason, I always think I can. Marty, "What's that?" Me, "It's the mug/trivet/coaster shelf. Thought I'd draw out what I'm thinking." Marty, "It's a square." Me, "Yeah, I apparently drew the aerial view."

I had to learn so many new things for the shop switch that I took to taking "dam" breaks, fingers firmly lodged in my ears. Not because I didn't want to hear new things (if that had been the case, I'd have been going, "nananananana" as well) but because my brain had been taking in so much new info during those months, I thought it wise to proactively try to prevent any leaks.

Just trying to get some things done and what should I hear but that witch I worked for going, "Oh my God! I got a paper cut! I did not sign on for no paper cuts. Totally not down for that." So yeah, she shut down the new shop build on that day. (Supervising is apparently hard work!) I kinda knew it was coming because she'd already said, after I got a lot done, "Who are you? And what did you do with me?"

Boy, do I wish I could do a New York accent so I could tell this story properly but since I can't, you'll just have to use your imagination. I was looking online for organic fabric so I could get some bandanas made up. I found one place with a good price but no way to order, figure out postage, etc., so I called. Guy answered, "Service Bay." I asked how to find out these things and he said, with an incredibly thick and impatient with my idiocy NY accent, "Ya see there at the bottom of the page where it says info@___? You write us an email about what you want and where you want it sent, then we'll give you the info." So, I emailed and got a response telling me to call. (Now, why didn't I think of that?!) I called back and again asked for customer service and this time I got something other than "Service Bay." I asked if I could buy directly from them and the lady said, "No." So I said, "That's too bad because I was wanting it for bandanas for my shop" and she said, "Oh, then yes." I said, perplexed, "Because it's bandanas?" And her accent thickened and softened with nothing but patience for my incompetent self when she said, "You know that's why they give you that business license, right, honey? So that you can shop wholesale." (Now, why didn't I think of that?!)

The challenge in trying to do something you've never done before is figuring out how to do something you don't know how to do. (Now there's some deep thinking for ya!) That's why it's so great to have supportive family and friends who say just the right thing when you start fretting, "What's new? You never know what you're doing. Uh wait, I meant..." But it was ironic as all get-out that I thought, when closing the bookstore, "Hey, why not open a t-shirt shop? That should be pretty straightforward," and then retrospectively, "What was I thinking?!" since the t-shirts were the biggest challenge of all the items I ever carried in my shop. First off, I bought myself some organic, made-in-America blank t-shirts (everything in my tourist shop was made in America and eco-friendly), because I originally thought to do press on demand so I could offer the full array of drawings. That meant learning how to print and press, which meant a printer, and a heat press, neither of which I had any extensive experience with, and let me tell you, there are just no words to describe how certain stages feel while learning a new skill through trial and error. Nope, not a one. Sounds, like Grrrrrrr cover the feeling much better. The printer kept insisting we feed it, clean it, give it rest periods. Guess it didn't get the message that it wasn't no union shop. Not to mention that it was a picky eater that would wait until you were done with cheap paper exemplars to decide to chow down on the expensive heat-press paper, after it distributed the color on the page in whatever way made it most appetizing to itself. (It apparently didn't like it when its red touched its green. And never mind all the time I spent creating the perfect brown, that I hit on after Marty crossed his eyes over the way-too-many variations I had computer-mixed and I said, "Oh, stay right like that while I do a quick mix since your eyes are the perfect brown for this!" The printer didn't care, it printed whatever brown it felt like.) Then one day it just wouldn't feed the paper and, after trying everything I could think of to get it to work again and deciding it probably wasn't going to (I mean really, it was off its feed so it was probably going to die), I figured I'd have nothing to lose by shaking it around (and so much to gain in frustration relief) so I did that and, out popped my favorite mechanical pencil. Geez, talk about jealous siblings (from the Printing Family)– one cannibalizing the other. I'd have fired it if I could have, that headache-generating employee from hell. In fact I was all ready to build a funeral pyre (I did say "fire" right?) and toss it on there and send it back to where it came from, if not for how much contracting out the work out would have cost. (Professional printers, they want to be paid what they're worth. Pfft!) Fortunately, Marty has a more patient temperament since my daydreams were moving from fire to tossing it through a window and seeing its guts strewn all over the street, inkblood everywhere, cars rolling over it, when he took over the task. But even for him there was a limit that he reached when the printer randomly mirror-printed so that the abbreviations for the individual Four Corners states were backwards, making it so we were down to one state, with New Mexico becoming Minnesota, and the rest just a mess. I knew it was bad when I heard him humming, "If I had a hammer…" Then it was on to learning how to heat-press. Staring down the gaping maw of a real scorcher not being my first choice of recreational activities, having to spend time figuring out heat settings and press times was not my favorite thing. We wondered who'd be the first to forget the parchment paper and heat the transfer paper right to the machine and, that award went to: me! *Taking a bow* No, no, don't get up to clap. Smoke rises, you know. I finally sat down and had a nice little chat with it wherein I informed it that yes, it intimidated me a bit, seeing as how it has the power to burn the hell out of me. Seems that melted its blazing hot heart, as right after that I pressed my first decent press, and was then pressing like an amateur. It was nice to be able to hear the "kabam!" sound it made every time it popped open as more celebratory, less the harbinger of doom. Nevertheless, no one was happier than I when we came up with a logo and all future tees were farmed out for silk-screening.

It's a family trait that we often short-circuit electrical devices, so I wasn't wholly surprised that week when I checked in with the laser etcher to see how progress was going there and her computer had crashed, behind about a week. Then I checked in with silk screener to see how it was going there and, her screen broke and she waiting for a new one. Then I checked in with the printer and he was replacing all the outlets in his place. Anyone looking for an equipment upgrade? Want to hire me on to break the old stuff for you? You don't even have to live here because evidently I don't have to be in actual contact with things to make them go haywire.

Give it up for the Five Man Electric Band and the last name Lord! I finally thought to go into the garage to check on Marty when he was making new shop signs one day. It was supposed to be a "we" project but I got a bit distracted doing something else so it became a "royal we" project and he was getting 'em done so I of course sang, "Signs, signs, everywhere a sign!" Marty, "Thank you, Lord, for thinking about me, I'm alive and doing fine."

It was really too bad that it was Thursday the 12th when I received my wooden sign letters in the mail and that night when I found that I had an extra "a" and was shy an "e" and therefore had to e-mail the company who made them, informing them of their error. Yep, saying it was just one of those Friday the 13th things, rather than, "Now that I flipped it the right way I can see that it's the correct letter" would have been so much easier on the ego when I had to write back and tell them the error was mine.

I made a new shop to-do list for both me and Marty once we'd completed the first one and left it on the counter. Marty, picking it up and reading it, "I see that witch you work for stopped by again. Did she at least bring doughnuts?"

The master of accidental art struck again! Marty came out to see a backboard I was painting and said, "That's really cool! How'd you get that color?" I said, "Oh you know, the usual way. I didn't like the way it was coming out so a little paint, a little water, a little more of a different paint, a little more water. Similar to how I got that great texture on that other piece because you didn't know it was wet when you went in and sanded." Looked great. So many layers on the thing it was bowing to the point I was afraid we wouldn't be able to use it, but it looked great.

Ah, the glues that bond. I spent a fair amount of time looking for eco-friendly, made-in-America glue (and hoping "natural" isn't code for "horse") to glue the pin-backs and magnets onto the backs of my wooden magnets and souvenir pins. There was lots of research involved and it was all very interesting but I do have to say, there was just something about the process of finding green glue that was totally at odds with the glue-sniffing ritual that made kindergarten so much fun.

We originally intended for the drawings for my shop to look like rock-art pictographs of Kokopelli and Happy engaging in modern-day activities; however, we couldn't quite get that down in a way we liked, so the drawings ended up being more a colorful folk art, which I assumed I'd be putting on ceramic mugs. However, when I went mug searching, the only ceramic mugs I could find were made overseas. Luckily, in the process of looking, I found a potter who makes beautiful eco-friendly and made-in- America ones, so I sent him one of the drawings of the colorful folk art to ask if there was a way we could make them work for my shop. He wrote back and said that he maybe wasn't the best way to go for what I wanted. Then I realized I had forgotten to include a note telling him that I meant just to use the outline for a stamp, and no strong colors. (How he failed to read my mind and understand, without explanation? Beyond me.) We did figure out a way to make it work, and that mug design would go on to be my logo design, but it did amuse me at the time: that someone was telling me that hand-thrown pottery might not be the best medium for designs that were inspired by the early history around here. Now, the mugs had an embedded stamp on one side (so superior to the surface stamp a ceramic mug would have had) that made it so if held in the right hand, you were looking at the design. The lefties in my family loved the mugs, but wished for left-handed ones so they too could be looking at the design when drinking, and so I wrote the potter and asked if he could put the stamp on the other side of the mug in my next order. (Now you know that yes, there is such a thing as a left-handed mug–at least there was in my shop. Lefties loved that.) When he sent me the invoice, I learned something cool: he noted it as the handle on the other side of the mug, not the stamp. And there it was right there, getting a handle on the difference between mass-produced and artisan. In the mass-produced world, you take a mug and put a stamp on it. In his world, you make a vessel, embed a stamp, and then put a handle on it. It would end up being the left-handed mugs that were the prompt for how he remembered me when I placed orders. (The request had made him smile.) When I placed one of those orders, he asked if I would like any. As part of my reply I told him that my Mom, our resident lefty, had died. He said, "There will be a lefty mug in the box to honor your Mom." People often came into my shop and said it felt really good in there. I'd say that was because everything in there was made by kind people, who took pride in their work.

Get a Life! No, not you. (Well, maybe you.) When I changed over the shop from bookstore to tourist shop and was trying to decide what I was going to be putting on the sign above the display window, what one would see from across the street that described what was in the store and would make them want to cross the street to come into the store, "Get a Life" sounded perfectly reasonable to me, as the drawings all had "get" idioms and were all about stuff you can do to live it up here, right? But Marty didn't think it would be read that way (huh?!), so he nixed it. I had to move on to other ideas but it was a challenge. It took such significant brainstorming that Marty finally asked, "Okay, and for round twelve of 'what is going on the sign' you are going to try and look at the world the way most folks do, correct?" Seems I needed to get a clue. Then maybe I'd get it. Maybe even get to "Get the Goods."

When making changes to my shop I was absolutely sure, more than once, that there was a future award out there in honor of Marty and me, and that it would be named the "Triple F Award." We had to re-paint the sidewalk sign when I switched over to a different shop so we used up some old chalkboard paint to do so. Then Marty chalked the new stuff we wanted written and drawn onto it and brought it up to the shop. The next day, we were both standing right by the thing saying good-bye when the first couple of raindrops started to fall, yet neither of us thought to bring it inside. I finally noticed it sitting out there in a heavy rain after a lightning strike made me look up a little bit later. (No, this is not the point where the Triple F's come in.) I brought it in and realized that, even though the chalk was definitely not going to make another day, there was just enough left to give us great outlines for painting over the chalk. Yep, Fortune Favors the Foolish: Triple F.

I was well-suited for a bookstore as I am an organized minimalist by nature. Not so much for a tourist shop, which required a more aesthetic approach. I ended up spending quite a bit of time trying to figure out one of my retail life's more pressing questions: how a minimalist like me was meant to "junk up" a shop, because yes, that was a suggestion I kept receiving. Lack of skills notwithstanding, I knew I needed to figure out a display for my Christmas ornaments. (And for doing so I'm pretty sure I ought to have gotten an award... possibly a Darwin award.) I mulled over that one for a while, while looking at the eco-friendly twisted paper I used to make the ornament hangers, because it's just my natural inclination to work with what I already have, and decided I could just tie it to the hooks in the top of the display case and hang the ornaments from it. It looked nice, too, until I showed up the next day to a demonstration of how twisted paper, when hanging in long lengths with weight and not enough knots, becomes untwisted paper, with ornaments sitting, not hanging, in the window. So, I tied some more knots into it and that looked nice, until the next day, when I learned that once you have enough knots, it becomes "twisting around and not landing where folks can see the etched front of the ornament" paper. Then I scratched my head and thought, "Since it's facing in, all I have to do is reverse the knot at the hook and it will face out." But, huh? Not. Then I looked at the hook and thought, "Twist the hook, then they will be facing out!" And, success! Mostly. If you didn't mind regimented-looking ornaments. It was finally determined that I am just constitutionally incapable of pleasingly cluttering up a space even if it's in my own best interest so my Mom volunteered to step up with ideas for that one and be my "clutter teacher." So poetic! I spent many a day helping her organize her stuff, so she was pretty gleeful about making me a list for how to disorganize mine. And, by her efforts, I ended up with a pretty window.

After the shop conversion was complete my folks wanted to do a photo shoot of all the changes. As part of the shoot, my Mom told me she wanted a picture of me using the heat press. I pointed out to her that it wasn't on. She said, "It's not like you never acted like you were working when you weren't, before." Fair enough.

I hate stickers. (Dislike is not a strong enough word. I have cleaned the adhesive off way too many things, way too many times.) I wouldn't have had stickers in my shop if my family members who love stickers hadn't convinced me. So, of course, what was my very exciting, never to be forgotten, first-ever item of our original designs I sold after changing to a tourist shop? Uh-huh.

Main Streeters. We'd get together and talk about all sorts of mundane things: the meaning of life, politics, religion. Then, once we've solved all the world's problems, we'd move on to the loftier stuff; like grodiest barf stories. All it took was a sleepless night for one of our number because their pupper barfed on their head in bed and we had hours' worth of future conversation. Then Main Street morning topic officially moved past best barf stories and on to favorite eating spots when we were teens. There's a natural progression in topics to be found in that somewhere, even if not to everyone's taste. (Ewww! There, I said it for you.)

An untimely question, answered! Before the prevalence of cell phones I (and many others–including tourists resetting for a new time zone) used the County Clerk's big outdoor clock to check the time; however, one autumn, it did not fall back. That kept throwing me (and many others) off, so I finally called and when the phone was answered by a rather harried-sounding employee, I said, "I'm sorry if I'm wasting your time but can you tell me why the clock isn't keeping proper time?" The employee laughed and said, "We're waiting for a cable to fix it. Cortez, America, where everything is always behind." Me (going with the obvious), "Except, of course, your clock."

What a great day it was for me, someone who comes in at under five-foot-two, when I had a tall person totally get it! I had a light bulb stuck in a socket at my shop so I asked my tall neighbor if he'd try to get it out for me. He said, "Of course I will. The entire purpose of the existence of tall people is to serve short people. Can you reach this for me? Can you reach that for me?" And he did. And since I didn't want him to think I'd ever take him for granted, not appreciate his contributions to the short, I made sure I had something else tall for him to do for me the next day.

Take it from me, telling the witch you work for that twitching her nose should only be used in the service of house-cleaning, a la Bewitched, because otherwise it gives her a resting witch face, is a bad plan.

One thing I learned about solicitors from my years in a shop is that they don't like it when you ask them why, if something is so cheap, they don't pay for it themselves. Go figure. And yeah, I meant that literally. I'd tell them to go walk around my shop and figure out what I'd have to sell to cover those "only" prices ("only 20 dollars…"), and then we could discuss our various definitions of the word "cheap" ("So, you want to sell me a cheap ad?"), which, as it turned out, was not a favorite synonym amongst advertising solicitors. When I suggested to one that if it was so cheap, he pay for it on my behalf, he took umbrage at my word choice. So I proposed, and we agreed, that if he'd stop saying only, I'd stop calling his publication cheap.

Whereas I viewed the relationship between the idioms and the drawings on our merchandise for Kokopelli's Getaways as just word-play fun, that was not always true for everyone else. On the front end of the tourist shop we were printing our own designs, and misprinted the rodeo one. I automatically said, "Guess that's a family freebie." (One of the beauties of coming from large families is being able to go forth with confidence when trying something new, secure in the knowledge that, if all else fails, you've got future gifts. In fact, our families were so accustomed to the practice that we no longer had to tell nephews and nieces that if sizes were too big for the greats they could use them as jammies or grow- intos because they'd reassure us that's what they were already planning since they were old hands at wearing t-shirts from us that fit perfectly–two or three years after we'd given it to them.) To which Marty said, "Really? You want to give 'Get off my back' to family?" Me, "It's not like anyone is going to take it literally." Then, a few months later, right when my Mom was a little tired of all of us fussing over her after a Parkinson's disease-related fall, she asked us to press a tote for her. Which one did she pick? You know it. Then it was the customers, "Well, she does love horses but she knows I think she can be a bitch, so do you think getting her something that says, 'Get on your high horse' is a good idea?" Or, "Do you think I can give the lazy guy the one that says, 'Get into gear' and act like there was no hidden message there?" So I did have to concede that while it was entertaining as all get-out to me, maybe not as much for all the recipients.

When I changed to a tourist shop I didn't have a set date for when I closed for the season. I mostly determined that by downtown activity and the weather. And some years were just easier to make a decision than others, like the year when the most exciting thing that happened all week was calling the business across the street to tell them to go catch their outdoor rolling clothes rack because the wind was blowing it down the street. And though watching the clothes flutter their way down the sidewalk and then watching an employee chasing after was quite entertaining, it was also a pretty convincing argument for it being time to call it.

One of the unexpected bonuses of having a Dad who wrote my shop computer programs for me was getting to write my own codes for inventory and create my own internal tracking numbers for gift certificates. Ascending order for mine? Nah. It was so much more fun to go with band names and song lyrics: 8 {days a week}, 2112 {for that Rush you get with your purchase.}, 8675309 (you know you just sang it), 10 {years gone}, 3 {times a lady} 1158 {two minutes to midnight}. Total bonus when the gift certificate recipients got the reference.

Early on, after my shop switch from bookstore to tourist shop, one of my favorite tourist moments went to–drumroll–the friend! A couple came in and were browsing around and the husband asked me what the Four Corners symbol was. I explained it to him, to which he said, "That's a riddle you put on your merchandise; nobody knows that." Their friend then walked in the door and the man said to him, "I have a riddle for you. Do you know what that is?" Friend, right on cue, "That's not a riddle, that's the Four Corners symbol. Everybody knows that." (I'm not even sure I knew that before I moved here, but really enjoyed the slack-jawed look on his friend's face.)

Nothing like almost getting mowed over by a lady who flew out of her car so fast, I hardly had a chance to get out of the way. Her face was beet-red, so I asked her if she was okay. She said, "Yeah, I'm fine, but there are too many red cars out here! I just tried to drive away in the wrong one. I was trying to get out of there before the actual owners thought I was trying to steal it." I told her not to worry, that I don't even drive and I've done that one. Not to mention that I went to the wrong house to meet with the seamstress who made my bandanas because evidently, white vans and blue trucks parked in front of a house are not limited to her house and when I told her about it, she told me that she should have warned me because she'd done the same on an overcast night, and didn't even realize it wasn't her house until the key didn't work.

Biggest difference between the bookstore and the tourist shop? I rarely had any non-English-speaking people in the bookstore. (Buying a book you can't read not really being a thing.) It's a bit awkward communicating over the language barrier, but ways can be found. I had a couple in and the lady was looking at t-shirts and she handed one to her husband and pointed to her back. He was shaking his head while he spoke and it was clear to me he didn't get what she was talking about. I motioned to the changing nook to tell her she could try the t-shirt on but she shook her head no, so I took the t-shirt and put the seams across her shoulders to check the fit like she was trying to get her husband to do. She thanked me by taking my hand and then pointed at Happy on the t-shirt and put her hand on her heart and smiled. No translator needed for that.

The thing about postal/package carriers is that you see the same person for years, have great little mini-conversations, and then their route changes and all of a sudden you don't see them anymore at all. A FedEx guy, a man who always made me laugh with his rather irreverent humor, got a new route over the winter so he was gone when I came back for the spring season. There were a number of temps in his place before another permanent route driver came on. Had one who knew the old driver so I said, "Please tell him hello for me and that I miss him." The temp driver looked at the electronic pad I'd just signed and said, "What's your name?" I said, "Roxanne, but I just sign first initial last name: R Lord." Temp guy, with an evil cackle, "Oh yeah, I will most definitely tell him that R Lord says hello and misses him."

I once read an article about how much our sales tax system annoys Europeans. They prefer their structure where the tax is included in the price, which was something for me to contemplate for my pricing, since a solid portion of my business was European tourists. So, I did the math and found that you can price something tax included at an even number, then back it down for the tax, but if you try to set the price so that with tax it will come out at an even number, it doesn't, because of the penny. (I was trying to make it work both ways so that Americans, who are accustomed to a separate tax, could see the original price.) You'd need a half penny to accomplish that and though Lord knows we've had enough half-assed presidents to put on one, we don't have one. So, I had to go with it's better to annoy Europeans at check-out, when they've already committed to an item, than try to deal with that dilemma at the end of every month. Then I just told the Europeans that it's like the metric system; too sensible for Americans to adopt it. Because really, who isn't happy to do it your way when they've just been told they are smarter than you are?

I warned them! (But they never listened.) It's just an annoying reality that when you own a small business, you're going to deal with innumerable (though I think gazillion comes close) sales and scam calls from people who know you're going to answer the phone. Some days I'd just hang up, and some days I'd be just bored enough to decide to view them as entertainment. On one such occasion, the scammer went right into his spiel, even passed on all the niceties. Now, I believe in fair play, so I interrupted him to tell him that since it was quiet in the shop at that moment I'd be happy to stay on the line, wasting his time with no sale at the end of it; just an opportunity for some amusement for me. He told me he could outlast me, and there would be a sale at the end. Challenge accepted, so every time he spoke, I talked over him, asking a bunch of random things. Then he'd pause, and I'd pause. Then he'd speak, and I'd speak over him again. He finally said, "What are you, twelve?!" then hung up on me. Score! Really, never try to out-annoy someone with many siblings.

As a shopkeeper, I totally needed a waistcoat so that every time I cast myself in the role of the White Rabbit, I would look the part. I had to do yearly compliance for my credit-card machine, assure the company that I was properly protecting people's information. They emailed me about it but I was in the middle of something else when I read it one year and then promptly forgot it. The consequences for not getting it done on time not being fun, when it struck me that I hadn't done it, all I could think was, "Oh dear! Oh dear! I shall be too late!" So I called (just in time) and ended up talking to a guy in Ireland. We got through all the major questions (a feat on its own since each of us was only pretty sure the other was speaking English, our accents were so thick to each other), then onto the easy stuff and the final question: the date. Wouldn't think that'd be a problem, would you? Except I'm someone that rarely knows it, which made it the hardest question of all. Gotta love creative people, though. The guy couldn't tell me the date (why? No clue. Maybe he was bored and just screwing with me), so I had to come up with it, and since I didn't have a calendar or any electronic devices to check (I called from an old-school landline.) I decided to just throw out a number and asked, "Is it May 29th?" He said, "You're one off." I said, "So, it's either the 28th" (with an unanswered pause, followed by a high note hum) "or the 30th." To which he jumped in and said, "Yes!" And we both did a verbal happy dance. Yep, we're all a little mad…

I paid city retail taxes for twenty-three years, each month signing my name under, "I hereby certify, under penalty of perjury, that the statements made herein are TO THE BEST OF MY KNOWLEDGE (caps are mine) true and correct." Which I much preferred to the state one that only said, "Signed under penalty of perjury in the second degree." The best argument ever against big government: the locals got that we are all ill-informed idiots sometimes, the state didn't.

Kokopelli's Getaways made sense to me as the name for my tourist shop, but not so much to the various other entities I had to deal with, as I was constantly having to correct their version of my business name. And though you might reasonably assume it was the "Kokopelli's" part that was problematic, no, it was the "Getaways." The most common error (and it was weirdly very common) was to call it "Kokopelli's Giveaways." Which doesn't sound all that bad, until you start imagining the idioms Marty would have been drawing for the shop: "Give a shit... Give a hard time... Give the evil eye... Give the finger." My goodness, had I given "Giveaways" a shot, I'd have definitely had to give up on word-of-mouth advertising. (Kokopelli's Giveaways? Yeah, they give you the shaft–nothing was free.) So, give me a hand, won't you, for not giving the nod to that one? Then I picked up another new name: "Kokopelli Gateaways." That one really didn't make much sense at first but then I thought about the sipapu (the hole in the floor of kivas. A portal [or gateway, if you will) from whence Ancient Puebloans are said to have emerged into this one) and "gateaways" created all-new possibilities. Kokopelli and Happy could gateaway to all-new dimensions. Maybe even do some planet-hopping. Happy and Kokopelli could be stars of other star systems. Alpha Centauri, here they come! With maybe a stop at Sirius along the way... a dog star for a major canis.

Though it was really convenient to have a theatre next door in order to engage in escapism, having a shopfront on Main Street meant I didn't really need to go to a movie to interact with those who occupied a different reality. It was a fine summer day when I had a man come into the shop and tell me he was an Anasazi seer, come here through a sipapu to warn us of upcoming events that would require that we seek shelter at Mesa Verde or Chaco Canyon or the like. He said he was seeking a dog because he'd been having visions that involved a dog and since I gave Kokopelli a dog, I must be an Anasazi seer, as well. I interrupted him to name Happy and introduce myself (first name only) and he responded by coming to shake my hand and to tell me that he only went by Lowman, his last name, because it represented where he fit into the Anasazi hierarchy. I tried to lighten the mood a bit by saying, "Oh, well, my last name is Lord, so I guess I'm at the top of the hierarchy. Haha." Oh my, did that ever set off a round of profuse apologies. Evidently, a Lowman is not meant to touch a Lord, and he wanted me to know that he would never have done so if I'd just had the foresight to warn him. (I'm apparently like every other boss out there: too short-sighted for the job, but carrying the title, anyway.) He took his leave of me then, but returned about a month later, right before the fall, to let me know that he was leaving town because its residents were all too stupid to save. He wished me luck with my mission (I couldn't be stupid. Remember, I'm a Lord on the hierarchy) but he'd decided everyone else was doomed and not worth his effort. And, he still hadn't found his dog, which was just further evidence that he was mistaken when he thought he should come here. I wished him well, and he bowed politely and left. Proof positive right there that there's no excuse for bad manners. If someone living in an alternate universe can execute good ones, so can you.

Seriously, people, if you're going to go up against ridiculous and win, you've got to have a sense for the absurd. I had a dog come into my shop once who was not what he was supposed to be: a "safe" breed. He was a rescue from a shelter and he definitely had some Beagle (acceptable to the human's landlord) but he also definitely had some Hound and Pit Bull (unacceptable to the human's landlord). His humans were savvy enough to get the shelter to list him as a Beagle mix so there was no paper trail of anything else but then they totally blew it with what they named him: Duke. I had to tell them, no one feels sorry for a Duke–or a Prince–or even a Baron. If you might end up getting threatened with eviction over your dog you want an entirely different name. "You don't like Oliver/ Huck/ Scout? Classic bully!" And no, calling the dog "Dookie" would definitely not fix that problem.

When I had to replace my credit-card machine because of the introduction of chips, my rep made the one-and-a-half-hour drive to Cortez to help me with it. I didn't technically ask her to come, I just said, "Okay, so when I get my new credit-card machine I can just plug it in and go and if I screw anything up, I should call you?" and she apparently had a flashback to my first machine. Funny, how one person's question is another person's threat. I then asked her if there was some secure way to dispose of the old one, preferably to recycle it somehow. She said, "No, the only secure way to get rid of it is to beat the crap out of it with a sledgehammer, then drive back and forth over it with your car until it flat-lines." And there ya go, the very reason she was my credit-card rep; no nonsense looking out for my best interests.

I was apparently putting out a vibe over how much I missed the bookstore sometimes, where I never had a credit-card machine and could just reach on a shelf for a good whodunit, because one day I was treated to "Kokopelli's Getaways and the Mystery of the Phantom Credit Card Machine." Let me tell ya, all that time I spent worrying about getting used to the new credit-card machine when they went to chip readers? Wasted, just wasted. Evidently, it was so easy I could have done it in my sleep, as I must have, since I was on a seasonal plan for my credit-card company so I wouldn't be charged for the months I wasn't open and yet I received a credit-card statement during a seasonal off month that showed transactions that took place while the machine was sitting in the box it came in. So, I called customer service and the guy said, "It's showing that they were swiped at your terminal." Me, "Well, I'm pretty sure no one broke into my shop, opened the box the machine is in, plugged it in, and swiped a bunch of cards in order to give me money." Guy, "You're right. Probably didn't happen that way." They decided the best way to fix that one would be giving me a new code, which was not, however, the resolution my machine would have preferred. It must have spent the rest of its time in the box stewing over the fact that I rejected its gift of free funds and set out to get revenge and settled on: treating my first actual credit-card sale as a return. (I knew right off that that couldn't be right because really, who in their right mind would return a Happy item?!) I could tell something was wrong by the way it spit out the receipt–with attitude. Some might think it was operator error (like the nice but irritated lady making the purchase), that I had pushed the wrong buttons, but I knew better; it was my credit-card machine, pushing my buttons. How dare I shove plastic down its throat when it had proven willing to register funds with no such indignities performed on its poor self? Had to be that, since for sure it wasn't because I had moments of incompetence that made that witch I worked for wonder why she hired me. I mean, really, was it my fault that my "waste not, want not" approach to office supplies, wherein it was my habit to let my credit-card paper run a few transactions into the pink sides that let you know it's getting low (there were like three transactions still there!) went a bit awry when I learned the paper size for the new machine was not the same as for the old, while a customer was waiting for their receipt? (And I'm just sure I could hear the new machine designers laughing their asses off, saying, "She thought the new machine would take the same paper. What an idiot!") I swear, had I not promised that machine to another small business when I closed shop I'd have been shoving a credit card so far down its throat it would've been printing messages begging me to run over it with a car. It was a happy day for me when I got to say, "Ba-bye, credit-card machine, may you rot in hell!

I am totally unclear as to why people even debate the reality of alternate universes, as the evidence is all around us. I sent an email to someone to see if they could do something for the shop for me that was entirely outside of my skill sets, but reasonably presumed to be within theirs. They turned me down because what I was looking to do was more complex than what they preferred to do, but so easy that I could do it myself. A small excerpt from their email, "I believe it is something that you are able to do yourself... Simpler ones I like to work on as it keeps my skills up." The other side of the veil, where you keep your skills up by only doing easy things. Why have someone pay you to do the hard stuff when they can just do it themselves?

I had an elder tourist couple stop in my shop whenever they went through town on their way to visit their kid. They liked to claim they were a bit shy but you couldn't tell it by me because, man, they often had me crying with laughter. On one occasion she said to him, "I don't have a bra on so, you need to try on this t-shirt to see if it will fit me." He went into the changing nook to do so and when he came out she grabbed the chest of the t-shirt and pulled it out (about three inches lower than a much younger person might) and said, "No, I don't think my boobs will fit in this. Nothing for it but you're going to have to go get my bra out of the car so I can try one on and be sure." Which he did, and returned with it in hand; raising it triumphantly because he'd managed to find it amidst all the travel stuff. She then found one that fit and he decided to buy the one he had tried on for her. About a week later I received a phone call from him. Seems he'd lost his somewhere between here and home and couldn't even try to accuse his wife of stealing it since we all knew her boobs wouldn't fit, and would I send him a new one?

Nothing like getting a monthly credit-card statement for a very small shop with fees (not even transactions) totaling $383,814.04. So I called the company. Service rep, "Yeah, that was an error." Me, "Ya think?" And we both got to start that day with a good laugh.

Overall, I would describe the neighbors I had on Main Street as the kindest, most good-hearted people you could find. However, with the natural rotations of businesses and employees there were a few, over the years, who strained my patience. And, not being one to sit quietly by when someone was being unneighborly, I'd open my mouth and be cast in the role of villain. (And there I was, thinkin' I'm all easy to get along with.) I occupied my shop for twenty-three years and for the first seventeen, there was never a problem with employees using the very limited parallel parking spaces on the street. Each understood the premium that businesses place on available parking. Then, what felt like overnight, that changed. We had people who'd received parking tickets greater than their hourly pay decide that the proper response to that was to either spray the chalk line with water or roll their tires. If I pointed out the dearth of available spaces they'd say that it was all wide open when they parked but somehow had no answer when I'd say, "And yet, you parked in front of my place and not yours." There just was no argument about common courtesy toward their neighbors they would hear, set as they were on proving that "Big Brother" held no sway over them. In fact, as it became more contentious, when I would say something to them I was told that I was the discourteous one for not minding my own business. (And yeah, the irony of that statement, when trying to mind a business was exactly what I was doing, went right by them.) I thought I got somewhere once when one of them told me, "Everyone can walk." Me, "Yes, the rest of us all walk." Them, "Everyone can walk. If there isn't a space, customers can walk. If everyone else's customers are unwilling to park farther away and walk, then you all just have crappy customers." (Never mind that it is a tourist town and many of us relied on people being able to make impulsive stops, they were a business that catered primarily to local trade, so no worries for them.) I finally had to call the out-of-state owners of one business, and they promised to lower the boom. Later that week, Marty was going through the shopping list, trying to decipher my handwriting, and asked, "Is that a lemon? What do you need a lemon for?" Me, "Because I want to suck on one, see if I can recreate the expression my Main Street neighbors who now have to park in the back get every time they see me." Marty, "Now, now, no reason to be snide. I'm sure the expression you're seeing is just thirst, a result of that looong walk around the block. I'll get some Gatorade you can give them." Then we headed out for our nightly walk, where I did some venting, "Geez, do these people think I like having to go from a polite request to 'I so love how people try to rationalize being a thoughtless ass?'" When we got back to the house I decided chocolate would be just the thing so, I opened up his Three Musketeers bag of mini-bars, took out three, and what did I find? Little sayings on them,

"You're awesome, Well-played, You slay." and thought to myself, "Now you're talkin'!"

Always such a treat, dealing with regulatory agencies. At one point, I was thinking about asking a friend to make dog biscuits for my shop (stamp Happy and Kokopelli into them), so I started looking up the legal requirements and, my word! I get wanting anything that's consumed to be safe but really, think about what dogs eat when left to their own devices. I decided that the next time I was at a friend's house and their dog was digging through the cat-litter I was so totally going to ask, "Is that cat shit certified?"

Just out of curiosity, I looked up Cortez on Wikipedia one day. The entry for it said, "The City of Cortez is a popular stop for tourists, who do not necessarily tour the city, but stay there because of its central location among surrounding attractions, such as Mesa Verde National Park, Monument Valley, and the Four Corners." And I thought, "That is so entirely us!" "Friendliest town in the West" (at least that's what the sign says) and folks only stopping to eat and sleep. What the entry didn't mention is that there is a little-known urban legend about Cortez that you won't be reading about in tourist guides (that would be because I made it up): we have a strange vortex that senses any weakness in motor-powered vehicles, causing them to break down for unspecified periods of time. We don't really advertise it (again, because I made it up), but it does get folks who might otherwise have driven right on through to stop and eat, stay at a hotel, buy something from local shops. Made a killing off it myself, many the day: people buying books, sweaty people needing a new t-shirt and maybe a bag for all the other stuff they'd be buying in town, some stickers to hold their car together and, maybe a notecard to thank the citizens of Cortez for our fine hospitality in their time of need. I'm rather fond of that vortex, myself. (Even though I made it up.)

Really, I should have been teaching sales courses. A VFW gentleman selling raffle tickets came in and asked, "Would you like to support Veterans of Foreign Wars?" and I said, "I like it just fine, been doing it my whole life. Well, except when I've been driving him nuts." (My Dad is a Vietnam vet.) Then I inadvertently demonstrated what that looks like by buying the tickets but then telling him he couldn't leave the shop until he looked around so he'd know what's in there and be able to tell other people. He did so, and then he picked up a mini-matchbox holder and brought it to my desk. I said, "You don't have to actually buy anything, you just have to look," and tried to take it from him. He pulled it back saying, "No, I want it." (Best salesperson ever, right here!)

A lot of shop-shifting went on downtown, where an established shop moved to another location. When it was the office supply store on the other side of the street from me they put up a big sign saying, "We're Moving! Look for us at our new location: 28 W. Main St." So, I was scratching my head trying to figure out where that meant they were going and finally realized that (duh!) as I was 29 West Main Street it would put them directly across the street from me; next door to where they were currently located. Now, while you are sitting there thinking, "How could she be so dense?" consider this: at the end of that week they put an arrow under the sign, and added the words, "next door." Seems I wasn't alone in my head-scratching.

The upside of the dance studio across the street putting in outdoor speakers was lovely music on Main Street. The downside was not realizing you were dancing to it until someone yelled out their car window at you, "Kick it, sister!!" If only I could actually sing and dance, a Main Street Musical could have been a thing.

I so love when people surprise me. I had a young adult male in my shop, full of swagger. He had a "gangsta"-style bandana wrapped around his head, all the points perfectly lined up on his forehead. I told him he should buy one of mine, have Happy and Kokopelli on his forehead. He said, "No way, I'd look like a dork." I said, "Come on back when you're badass enough to look like a dork." He just looked at me for a minute and then said, in a serious tone, "I'll do that." And, a few months later, he did. He must have channeled the badass elder from Tokyo I had shortly before he came back in. That gentleman didn't take any convincing at all. He saw my bandanas and said, "A dew claw do-rag–I am all over that!"

Who knew there could be so many theories on window crackage and so many experts to put them forth? I had a small crack in my display window that, after eighteen years, finally traveled to the point that the theatre had to replace it. While awaiting the new pane we used duct tape, on the advice of glass people, to hold it together. The duct tape drew so much interest I seriously considered it as a future advertising approach. People would come into my shop to ask about it and then tell me their theory on what had cracked the glass. (It actually ended up being fun, to hear how each interpreted it based on their own primary world view: the cop who thought it was a BB gun, the construction worker who thought it was a rock kicked up by a vehicle, my neighbor who thought it was the downtown bat, etc.) Turns out it was just that the glass wasn't properly secured because one of the fasteners had slipped and it had been shaking in the window for all those years and finally just gave out. Not as exciting maybe as the proposed theory that it was the horn from a semi that blew through it but hey, that one sounded good, anyway.

It's true that, at times, Cortez lacked the hustle and bustle that one might associate with a downtown area, but what we lacked in volume, we tended to make up for in character. One day, when returning to my shop after using the theatre offices' facilities (no, a restroom never magically appeared in my shop, so I always had to run upstairs) I was stopped by a guy about my age looking in my shop window who said, "Have you seen these? These are so cool! I love Kokopelli!" Then he showed me the gigantic Kokopelli ring he was sporting on his finger. We chatted a bit, and while we were talking a young guy walked past with a fast-food restaurant uniform top slung around his shoulders. Guy my age stopped him and said, "I know that shirt. Do you know <named a certain woman>?" Young guy, "Yes, I just moved here, and she's been really great!" Older guy, "That's my wife." Old guy and young guy then fist-bumped and gigantic Kokopelli ring met giant whatever ring young guy was wearing and "Clash!" metal on metal rang out strong. I looked at them and said, "Wonder Twins Power!" Older guy, "Activate!" Young guy looked bewildered, said, "Okay, I'm definitely not in Detroit anymore." Older guy, "No worries, you'll love it here." And off they wandered together. A few months later, I learned to never underestimate the real, observable, and verifiable power of Wonder Twins. Yep, I saw both the big-ring guys at different times and in different places and they were both wearing black cargo pants, similar t-shirts, and biker head scarves. (That's what I'd say when talking to bikers, "Love your head scarf!" Drove them nuts.) Kokopelli ring met whatever ring, and they are now forever destined to be somehow connected.

The Cortez Fire Protection District took my Mom's blood pressure once a week for I don't know how long, but a few years, at least. Almost every time they did, they gave her a refrigerator magnet. (Pretty big ones. My Mom never said no to any kind of gift. She considered that rude. And she loved getting things like that.) They were, for a time, my neighbors downtown (administrative offices) while they were having a new building constructed. After my Mom died, I found a huge stack of their refrigerator magnets and I thought they might appreciate having them back so I kind of snuck over there one day and dropped them on someone's desk. When they were moving to their new space, I was outdoors at the same time as one of the muscular firefighters when he was carrying a box out, handling it like it weighed a ton, and in it I could see the magnets. I remarked on them, something like, "Wow! A stack like that is heavier than you think when it's magnets," and he said, "Yeah, they just appeared out of nowhere one day. Don't know how someone managed to lug them in without us noticing, but nice surprise!" Flexed my guns when I got back in my shop, oh yes I did.

And, in a clean sweep. One of the new employees at the theatre (they had pretty high turnover, as kids graduated from high school and moved on, so I met new ones all the time) did something rude in front of my shop and we were talking about it while he was sweeping. He said, "I'll tell you what. I'll do you the favor of sweeping your sidewalk." I said, "Sweeping OUR sidewalk is your job, not a favor; it's only a favor when I do it." He said, "I didn't know that. Don't I at least get credit for offering?" I said, "Okay, but you're still down one since offering is nullified by not knowing your job." (The look he gave me! Still makes me laugh.) And he wasn't alone. I had a really good first day back after a seasonal break, to include neighbors stopping by to welcome me back, check out the changes. Which, once I thought about it, made it their fault; that I so totally misjudged what was coming next. Yep, theatre employee came by, someone I knew because they were there before I took my little break, and I was thinkin' they came by to welcome me back too, but no, they came by to ask if they still had to sweep my sidewalk, since I was back and all.

Just a little retail dilemma. My shop faced north, so I didn't really get any direct sunlight. Nevertheless, indirect sunlight can cause t-shirt fading but, as far as I could see, not too quickly, so I assumed I could get in a full tourist season before I needed to switch things out. However, I had to reevaluate that conclusion after a lady came in and asked where I had the "gray" t-shirts, "like the one in the window." (I didn't carry gray t-shirts.) After she left, I was standing on the sidewalk contemplating how it could have looked gray to her since it certainly looked black to me when my neighbor came by, so I explained the gray remark to her and asked if she thought it was time to change them. She said, "Oh, you can wait to change them. That person must have been color-blind, they are obviously dark brown." Me, "Right?! Except they're black." Then I was stuck wondering if I should change them because they were faded, or just treat them like a computer screen: "Colors might not be as they appear... to you."

Small business owners, looking out for each other by doing the absolute opposite of baiting and switching. (Subtitled: My life in amusing emails.) Me, to a rather terse artisan who made items for my shop, "What's the minimum order for the standard size and what do they cost?" Artisan, "You don't get the standard size, you get the mini." Me, "Yes, but I'm thinking about trying the standard size and would like to know how many and what they cost." Artisan, "Oh, okay, x amount for y." Well, phew! I was really looking forward to carrying that item so it was good to know that him saying, "You don't get the standard size..." wasn't a declarative statement, just a helpful reminder. Also good because I didn't want to have to ask his CEO (Chief Entertainment Officer) and winter foot warmer, Scout, to intervene. (One of the ways I chose the artisans I contacted to work with was by the info on their websites, and that's how he described his dog on his. Made me smile.)

Another sole proprietor, "I'm just drowning in paperwork!" Me, "Right? And as if the run of the mill is not enough, that witch I work for tried to make me sign an NDA. Not, of course, about sexual harassment or discrimination or the like since, you know, hurting me in such ways would for sure put the hurt on her, but she did try to demand that I hold my tongue about things she thought only she should be able to speak about. And so I held my tongue, but that made her tongue-tied, and she thus claimed that had been a slip of the tongue and that I must loosen my tongue lest she continue to sound like she was speaking in tongues." (Just a little tongue in cheek.)

Ritual and tradition, maintained! When my shop was a bookstore, my desk was by the window and people who knew where to look could easily see me inside and thus, for many years, I got a friendly wave from the mail carrier when he didn't have time to stop; a light tap on the glass to get my attention if I wasn't busy with someone but didn't see him. When I changed the shop over I moved my desk across the room, where I was not as easily seen, and the mail carrier, concerned that he might interrupt me in the middle of something that he couldn't see, stopped tapping and waving. I told him no worries on that front; the mail carrier tapping and waving is part of the small-town tourist experience for many. And he went back to tapping and waving. Because really, what's a small town without a friendly wave from the mail carrier?!

Why yes, I am pedantically annoying about certain things. The Post Office raised the rates on postcard stamps so while I was there, I decided to get penny stamps to add to the ones I kept at the store for customers, but I couldn't remember how many I needed so defaulted to my lower guess and said I'd be back if I was wrong. Postal lady (all the folks at our post office have always been nice people, with good senses of humor), rolling her eyes, "It's only a penny." Me, "If a million people spend an extra penny a day that's ten thousand dollars, a day, for services not rendered. Today you'll have to settle for nine thousand nine hundred ninety-nine dollars and ninety-nine cents." Big head shake from postal lady but I didn't hear her offer to pay for it in my stead, now did I?

There are certain words you are just as happy to not hear strung together in a coherent sentence when you are taking receipt of your tax return for review before submitting it, like, "There's a high probability that you will tick the right algorithms to prompt an audit." I was so glad, then, that my Dad (retired CPA with a Master's in tax) added that reassuring part about, "You might get lucky, and someone might actually look at the form before contacting you." Nevertheless, that little add-on did have Dirty Harry in my head asking, "Are you feeling lucky, punk? Well, are you?" so I did decide that it might behoove me to change the name of my tax-file icon because it occurred to me that "taxes-shortcut" might just be misinterpreted by certain interested parties. ("No, really, that's not me shorting you on your cut. That's a default name.") And then, that while I was at it, I'd probably need to do away with the "Books2" one too, or someone might come along looking for my second set and not buy that that it was just a back-up file.

I never think I'm bossy but then I sent a query to a small business I'd been working with, which they answered in the affirmative, and I wrote back and said, "Then I would appreciate it if you would...." (and listed the things I'd like done) and they wrote back to say, "OK!" (I blame that witch I worked for. I was only writing what she told me to, after all.)

It was quite the experience when I dropped in on a business board meeting where one of the main players couldn't stand me, and expressed their displeasure at my presence by making faces when I was speaking. (Adulting, much?) I left saying, "I almost said thank you for allowing me to attend but since you didn't actually have a choice, I'll say thank you for the time." Then I went home and emailed them asking for the date and time for the next meeting, you know, just so they'd really look forward to it.

I figure small children and pets have something in common; they'll let you know if they want to interact with you. Both were welcome in my shop, and I generally let them approach me, unless their behavior caused me to approach them. And so it was with Punk, a dog I met when he came in with his humans. He wasn't much interested in making my acquaintance but not doing so wasn't an option, since he wasn't one of the better behaved, so I played my trump card on him and said, "Punk, I am LordPunc (short-form combo of my and Marty's last names), which means, I outrank you. You will hereafter do whatever I tell you." And it worked! (Not.)

And then there was Reggie, "Oh my God, oh my God! You're letting me in? To the secrets of store? I always wanted to know what was in store! I love you, I love you, I love you! Let me see! Let me see everything!" (Every word clearly enunciated by the happy swish of a tail from a great big Airedale plus pupper.)

I can't imagine anything that will ever replace my favorite, "Difference between Americans and Europeans?" generalization I heard once, and used often in the shop, "Americans think two hundred years is a long time and Europeans think two hundred miles is a long way," but you can also tell the difference when it comes to bags. I maintained the same habit with merchandise bags for the tourist shop that I had for the bookstore; I'd ask someone if they wanted one, not just hand one to them. Now Americans, they came into the store and commonly rejected the totes by saying, "I already have more bags than I know what to do with" but then would accept a disposable bag to carry whatever they purchased–even on those occasions when it was a bag. Europeans, on the other hand, tended to like the totes, and almost universally laughed when I asked if they wanted a bag–for their bag.

It's not like downtown businesses don't stay au courant (pardon my French) on employment issues so yeah, it was a topic of conversation when prospective employers started demanding social media email and passwords as part of the interview process so that they could log in as you and review your activity. That, of course, created another sole-proprietor multiple-personality-disorder moment brought to me, and me, by employers. Roxanne, "So, you want to work in my shop? Hand over your password." Roxanne, "Not happening, that's private info you have no right to." Roxanne, "You're not hired!" Roxanne, "You can't not hire me, I already work here." Roxanne, "Then you're fired!" Roxanne, "Fire me and your business is going down. Just sayin'."

That day when: my "Get Lit!" motto became a more universal theme. You might fairly assume that a town with drive-through liquor stores would be relatively relaxed on the idea of legal pot, but not so much. Recreational marijuana sales was a pretty hard-fought issue in Cortez, with some of the most vocal opponents to legal weed often being some of the heaviest drinkers in town; which is why I determined that if I was looking to open a pot shop, I'd totally put it next to a liquor store and name it, "The Pot Calling out the Kettle," with maybe a directional arrow on the logo. Arguments against notwithstanding, there did come a day when I guessed I was going to have to learn what the pot-related equivalent to "dry" was because when Cortez went "yes" on recreational marijuana sales in the city limits, we became the closest legal pot... the gateway, if you will... for three dry states. Shops practically flew up overnight and I remember thinking, on the day we hit four pot shops, that it was really helping with walking traffic, now that high season had a whole new meaning, and that I really hoped one of the next pot shops would open next to a drug-testing center. Such a photo op for tourists! We were all adjusting to the changes in town when I overheard a hilarious miscommunication between two people outside my shop that made me realize there were more adjustments needed than most anticipated. The law also allows for growing personal weed and so, as a result of that conversation, I had to tell my friends, "You might want to find a different way of saying your garden has gone to pot, or weed. You might even want to watch how you phrase talking about the skunk in your yard, 'cause you might have someone inviting themselves over for no reason that you can readily grasp." For myself, I must have looked rather "pot-friendly" since I was just racking up the tourists asking me where they could buy it, if in rather hushed tones, like the one lady I had who mistook the cop shop next door for a marijuana shop (that must have been a surprise when she walked in), and then determined she could use a little guidance. Eventually, I decided I needed a sign that said, "I will gladly give you directions to the nearest marijuana shop. And I will happily engage in whatever conversation you'd like while you are working up the nerve to ask me. But, this is Colorado. Not only do I not care why you want it (I'm not your mother, your priest, or your doctor), the law doesn't care either." Then, in a plot twist I certainly never anticipated, I had to add a postscript saying, "Unless it's pickles." Yep, there I was, directing people to the nearest legal pot–and there was Marty directing people on how to get homegrown pickles on the sly. People who probably didn't even know they wanted to know how to get illicit pickles until they learned that in Colorado you could buy legal marijuana, but if you wanted homemade pickles, not made in a commercial kitchen, you'd have to get them off the back of a truck. So yeah, the more daring amongst us could still live on the contraband edge here... by buying black market pickles. And no, I'm not going to tell you how because for all I know, you could be a narc.

"They aren't round." (Just thought I'd let you in on the second-most-common comment about the best-selling hand-thrown mugs I carried in my shop. The very cool, and not perfectly round, mugs. Who'da thunk that would be such a pleasant surprise to folks?)

Okay, then. I had a gentleman walk in the door, put on a cap, and walk over to pay for it, telling me, "It fits!" I said, "Perfect! But there is a slider in back so that the size can be adjusted if need be." He said, "No, the determining factor for me is if it already fits. If it does, I buy, if not,

I don't." Then he stayed for a while to tell me all about how he's a good traveler because he's so adaptable. Mmmmhmmm.

Leave it to kids to get the unspoken tag lines. A lady and her son were standing on the street, obviously waiting for someone, freezing, so I went out and invited them into the shop so they could warm up a bit. They browsed around and the son was ooohhhing and aaahhhing and the Mom finally said, "It's not like you haven't seen Kokopelli before." Son, "But he has a DOG!" I laughed and said, "Yes, he does. The dog's name is Happy." Kid looked at his Mom, "He has a dog named HAPPY!!!" Two minutes after they left, kid was back to buy.

It's hard sometimes for me to describe people in writing, so that they can be seen as I see them; the generosity of spirit that shines through their hardships. Notwithstanding, I'm going to give it a shot. I had a lady who stopped by and visited me at the shop on occasion for many years. A sober alcoholic, but as she said, the alcohol did a lot of damage before she became sober. When I was a bookstore she would bring me random books every now and again. She didn't want to sell them to me, just wanted me to have them. When I changed to the tourist shop she came by and asked me to set aside a t-shirt that had an embroidered Kokopelli and Happy design on the sleeve for her to buy and then came back once a month or so to tell me how saving up for it was going. (I'd have given it to her, but saving for it, from the little money she earned at her job, was important to her.) She came back a while later, after she bought the first, to ask me to set another one with the design on the sleeve aside. I had by that time switched to a silk-screened chest design, and offered to set aside one of those, if she preferred. She told me that she liked the old ones and would rather have one of those because she'd had a very hard year, and learned that petting the dog on her sleeve helped settle her. Now, one of the things I learned early on when speaking with her was that she no longer made the connection to unintended humor, so when she'd say something I might find funny, I couldn't laugh, because she'd think I was laughing at her. But, I just couldn't help myself when she said, "I'm so glad you still have the old ones, because with the new ones, I'd be petting my chest." Yep, I laughed. She said, "Oh, that is funny, isn't it?" Then she laughed too. Just priceless, those moments.

The mail carriers on my shop route would always stop and chat for a minute when they had the time and I wasn't busy. One of them and I were of an age, and if I was cranking the tunes, he'd stop me from turning them down so he could rock out for a minute too, but he was also one who thinks it sad for anyone to be stuck in past eras for music (yes, I'm one of those) so he loaded up his phone with a new song every now and again he wanted me to listen to, to try and get me into the modern age. The last try was a cover of an old school song. He figured since I'm tone-deaf, I might not notice, and he could slip a new band right on by me. Sneaky, and busted! Just his bad luck that he chose one of my favorite songs, so I definitely knew the difference. He gave up after that and just went with whatever I was playing; that is, until the day he realized that he was delivering a check to me from my very first mail-order customer. Then he turned on his own tunes and did a happy dance for me... and I totally rocked to his music with him.

To hear the tales a blush could tell! I had a Doc from the Midwest in my shop and he was having a good time looking at the inventory and then he shook his head and said, "To see into the minds of the people who come up with this kind of thing." (With a bit of a tone suggesting he wasn't expecting what he found there to be quite right.) Me, "What would you like to know?" Doc, "You don't just buy this stuff?" Me, "No, you're looking at my and my husband's brainchild." Bright red, his cheeks went! I have no idea what he was thinking but I'd have definitely liked to see into his mind at that moment.

It is such a tiny, topsy-turvy world. I had an older lady in the shop from the East Coast one day who came in to ask me where the nearest pot shop was. Then she looked around a bit and an item of my inventory looked to her like something they made where her kid worked and through the course of small-world conversation we realized that was because, well, it came from the place where her kid worked, and that I had actually spoken with her kid. It was a total coincidence that she walked into my shop, she had no idea that connection existed; a coincidence that had her wishing she hadn't told me that she came to Colorado to smoke a big fat one (this was shortly after recreational marijuana became legal) before we figured out I was connected to her kid. She asked me not to tell the kid. I told her I wouldn't narc her out to her kid since, "It's none of my business what anyone buys unless I'm the one selling it." She then bought something so we could both tell her kid that we met while conducting what was my business.

Discussion between couple overheard at my shop, "You should buy a 'Get a Dirty Look' sticker. You love to quad." "Yeah, but that's not like my quad." "Excuse me? Did you notice that dog isn't like your dog either but you were all happy with it. Which one is a member of the family?!" "Uh...."

One of a non-salesperson/salesperson's favorite things? The problem-solver! Husband, "I wish I hadn't bought that t-shirt before we came here because I like these better but I really don't need any more." (Me thinking, "Me too!") Wife, "But, you didn't buy a hat." (Me thinking, "Yes! I really like her!")

"Do you live here?" Now there's a question–while I was sitting behind my desk–at my very small shop. "Uhm, do you mean physically? Is this where I sleep? Philosophically? Like this is where I spend a lot of the hours in the day?" Person, "No, do you live in this town? I need directions." Me, "Nah, I'm just visiting the franchise." (Yes, I gave them directions: highly detailed directions.)

I think we've all had the experience where it felt like fate put the right person in our path at the right time. I had a couple come into the shop because their car broke down when they were near town (Cortez vortex, that makes people's cars break down, strikes again!) and they were wandering around to kill time. They were Kokopelli and pupper lovers, so my shop appealed to them. Over the course of conversation I learned that she was trying to adjust to some emotional challenges related to a parent with Parkinson's disease. My Mom having had young-onset Parkinson's disease, I was able to give her a new way to look at it, without being nearly so hard on herself. She cried, so hard that her husband worried that maybe that conversation wasn't such a good thing. She said to him, "No, it's okay." Then turned to me and said, "I never thought I'd hear myself say I'm grateful that our car broke down at a most inconvenient time in a most inconvenient place but I so truly am." Me, too.

Take it from me, I was a marketing wonder! The FedEx guy waved at me whenever he walked by the shop. If he was parked out in front, he'd do a final wave as he was pulling away. I always waved back and one day that wave, coming from the open doorway where I was standing, caught the attention of a couple of tourists. They saw that wave but not the FedEx guy and thought I was waving them down so they came rushing in to make sure there wasn't an emergency and I wasn't choking on a chicken bone or something. Me, "No, I'm all good, just waving to the FedEx guy, but thank you so much for coming in to check. And by the way, are you familiar with who Kokopelli is?"

Something that anyone who has ever worked in retail can tell you: there is truly just no way to make some people happy. "This t-shirt is too much like a t-shirt." Uhhh-huuuh. I had to say, with the uplifted palm shrug, "What can you do? T-shirts being all true to themselves and such."

After the crash in 2008 things just virtually stopped downtown for a while and I'd have what I called "dreaded days" when no one came through my shop door. On one occasion the UPS guy came to drop off packages for the theatre and woke me up. Then he'd remark on it all the time like, "Oh, you're awake. Is this a no-nap day?" Fast-forward to 2020 when the pandemic hit and Marty was working out of our spare bedroom. There came a day when Marty came out of the spare bedroom for a break in the morning to find me dozing, and then he came out of the spare bedroom for a break in the afternoon to find me dozing. He asked, "Two naps, in one day?" So I had to ask, "What are you, the UPS guy, now?"

A day in the life: I answered the phone and had a man start talking a million miles an hour, "Kokos-what?! When'd you start calling yourself that? Never mind. This is so-and-so and you need to tell so-and-so that this-and-that are going on, need to be taken care of." (I try to interrupt.) "No, no, don't interrupt, I need this all done yesterday and I don't need any more problems. (Lays out all the stuff that needs doing.) "You got all that?" Me, "Yep, every word. Sorry to have to tell you though, you've still got a major problem on your hands." Man, "Good God, what now?" Me, "I don't know who you are, I don't know who so-and-so is, and you just wasted about five minutes of time you apparently don't have talking to the wrong number." Evidently, getting all that off his chest was enough to settle him down some, he then spent another five minutes grilling me on who I was and what my shop was all about, and then later came by to check it out.

I had a lady I'd never met before come in one day, apologizing for not having been in earlier. Then she went through and told me, very specifically, everything she liked about the merchandise. I'm not exactly sure why, but, since she had a lot of nice things to say, and told me she thought I was going to have a really good season, she was welcome back any time.

Just in case you were unaware, you are (almost) in the company of the extreme coolness that is me. Yep, yep, I became extremely cool to pot-seeking tourists because I could answer questions about Colorado pot law even though I wasn't smoking it. (I didn't know the two were mutually exclusive. Huh! Must have lost the brain cells that tell you that many years ago... poof... like a puff of smoke.) I have to admit, my initial response was to tell people to just ask at the pot shops but then I decided it would be helpful for me to know, so I looked the details of the law up online and then called a local pot shop to confirm my understanding. I was then glad that I had taken the time for the online check since I got such a brain-scrambling convoluted answer there, I was tempted to light a doobie, myself. I later groused to Marty about my inability to get a proper answer and he said, "You called a pot shop looking for a concise answer? You got just what you deserved." Point, Marty–and all the people who asked me instead of the pot shops. Then my entrepreneurial side kicked in and I started writing some basics on the backs of stickers so I could earn a little profit off all that info I kept dispensing. And yeah, my "Get Lit" sticker was the favorite choice for that one.

It's a safe bet, that the Dad I saw drop to his knees on the sidewalk on my side of the street after almost seeing his toddler run into traffic, decided it was worth the effort to walk a half block to the light from then on. He and his wife and toddler were at a shop across the street and when he left, he crossed midway through Main Street, which is also a highway. His toddler then came running out of the shop and tried to run after him. His Mom caught him just as he stepped into the street and his Dad, who had witnessed it all from too far away to intervene, experienced knee-buckling relief. I totally don't get why people jaywalk on highways. You versus vehicle; you are just never going to win.

We had a mountain lion cruising around town at the time that the Cortez Police Department had a satellite office next to my shop and the cops there knew I walked back and forth to work, so one of them came by and advised me to make some racket while I was walking. Since I didn't habitually walk around with bells on, we problem-solved that one until I suggested I could sing. The cop thought that a great idea, since he's heard my singing, but did hope that the mountain lion wouldn't think I was one of its own kind, caught in a trap. (Yes, I can yowl with the best of 'em, thank you very much!)

I'm pretty sure that after twenty-three years of seeing tweens flirting while leaning on the ledge below my window going into or out of the movies I should have a degree in anthropology: the dating rituals of young Americans. It was very consistent; young guy trying to work up the nerve to put his arm around young girl, he caaan't quite get there so he tugs on something instead (her hair, ear…), she pushes his hand away, they get into a hand-wrestling deal that ends in them holding hands. This very sweet reminder of your youth brought to you from the other side of the glass.

When Pokémon Go became a thing, the theatre kids gave me a heads-up that I had a Pokémon character at my shop. Now, there were a few folks who complained about all the "slow Pokémons" (Get it? Slow-pokey, mans) walking around, holding up traffic. Me? I thought it great that it was causing people to walk around the community, learn what's there, stop to talk to people they didn't know. So I had to tell a little cluster that I knew were Star Trek fans, "Come on now, folks! If you'd be logical about this, you'd totally admit that if the Next Generation of

Pokémon Go was 'Star Trek Boldly Go' you'd so entirely be out there engaged in tossing tribbles to catch characters, sacrificing red shirts, walking around saying 'fascinating'. Make it so, Nintendo!"

Merchandise sighting! Shortly after I switched over my shop I crossed paths with a man wearing a hat from my shop and said, "You're wearing my hat! Cool!" He backed a bit away from me and said, "What?" I said, "Your hat, it's from my shop." He looked a little relieved that I wasn't actually going to try to take it right off his head and said, "It was a gift. From your shop? It's great!" We then had ourselves a nice little chat. A definite change from the bookstore, where I had no way of knowing what came from me, so I wasn't accosting innocent people going about their business. But how could I not? So exciting to see Happy cruising around on someone's head.

One thing you can say for small-town people is that they aren't nosy, and they wouldn't dream of interrupting you when you're going about your business. That's why, when a bunch of orange cones went up next to my shop, people didn't go over and ask the folks at the place they went up in front of what was going on, they came into my shop and asked me; because it's not being nosy and interruptive as long as the people who actually know what's going on are not being asked. Nope, that's just making conversation. So much conversation that I finally had to go ask. The fire department administrative offices were moving in while their new administration building was being built and the cones were to preserve the parking spots for the moving van bringing their stuff over. You're welcome. Uh, I mean, they were.

I looked up from my desk in this here Wild West one day and there was mounted patrol on Main Street! I hadn't known they were going to be doing that, so imagine my surprise when I saw a helmeted head go by my shop and couldn't at first figure out why it was several feet above

101

where the average head might go by. Four horses there were, prancing down Main Street. Still, I was pretty sure it was not a harbinger of the apocalypse, even if there was a political debate that night.

Boy, could that witch I worked for ever be petty! She was acting like a corporate CEO one day so I said, "You ain't the boss of me!" and she retaliated by making me get an employee number so I would remember my place. I went with 6024377, the exact numbers we used on our old school calculators that, when turned upside down, read "go2hell." And young people think they invented text language. Pfft.

We all gotta get our kicks, somewhere. It was a constant battle, trying to get people who flew down Main Street on their bikes and skateboards to understand the danger they posed to other people (most particularly the very young and very old). So yeah, I got some satisfaction out of watching that badass who was riding his skateboard down the sidewalk, drinking his pop and trying to look all casual, run into a bigger badass: the little rock lodged in some sticky stuff. Abrupt stop for the skateboard, not the rider or his pop. He didn't think it at all funny, thought I was kicking him while he was down. But since he wasn't injured, I most certainly did.

Everyone on Main Street was very glad when the word started getting out about not leaving dogs in hot cars. No more trying to track down their people or find a way to get water to them through cracks in windows. One day I had a man just wandering around in front of the shop so I went out to ask if he was okay. He said he was waiting for his family, who were in watching the movie without him because they didn't have anywhere to bring their dog and he didn't want to leave him in the car, even if it didn't feel altogether hot that day and he was parked in the shade. I offered water for the pupper and air-conditioning for them both if they wanted to come into the shop. Pupper came in and napped on the floor, man and I had a nice chat until I closed, family presumably enjoyed the movie. All good.

When you're a small business owner, you spend a lot of time talking to government agencies and no matter what it's about, it's never their fault, unless it so obviously is, it's inarguable. I enrolled in a new online retail sales-tax program and it had a glitch that made my final payment three cents off from the payment-due amount, even after the final screen showed a correct total amount. Some might think (certainly the first person I talked to, did) that it's only three cents, but it was my three cents, so yeah, I gave them my three cents' worth about how I wasn't going to pay incorrect taxes, that if it was my error they'd hit me with fees for it, and that if they didn't correct it, it'd be on them if I paid my taxes late. They said they'd look into it and call me back and when I did not receive any such return call, I tried to call back, a number of times, and kept getting a recorded message. My final message must have sounded really pissy, since it prompted a senior software engineer to call me. He was a nice man, who offered up a cell-phone number that I could use "at any time." I told him I appreciated it but that I think people have a right to a life and I didn't need to be able to reach him at any time, I just don't like to waste my time over phone calls not returned in a timely manner. I later told that to Marty and he said, "Guess he learned he was talking to the person who, when asked by another city agency who had stood you up once before, what would be the best time to stop by (meaning morning or afternoon, nothing more specific), said, 'between 10:20 a.m. and 10:35 a.m.'" What? People have a right to a life, me included. And, props to them for recognizing that and making it in that time frame.

That moment when: you learn what it's like to be "rich on paper." Granted, it was only because I erroneously clicked on something when preparing my end-of-year tax books that somehow made a bunch of extra zeroes appear but hey, still rich on paper! Of course, once I started scrolling from assets to liabilities it also gave me extra negative zeroes there, but if you think about it, that meant: I made a bunch of other people rich on paper, too! I'm just generous that way.

I was so totally not down for it when big businesses started calling everyone "family" but that witch I worked for loved it! In fact, she showed up at our house and tried to make me do things! Work things! Getting-something-done things! And I almost did it. Thank goodness I remembered, just in time, that it's MY house, and I enjoy feeling underwhelmed and overappreciated. That I'm the boss of me, here. And so I got her to bake me some brownies before I kicked her out and lay down on the couch.

I was out on the sidewalk yakking with the Fire Chief one day while their offices were being redone and they were my temporary neighbors and he said, "Downtown has changed a lot since the mid-nineties when I was doing fire inspections." Me, "That was you? I can't say I thought about fire extinguishers much until you came by my shop. Now I have them everywhere." Fire Chief, "Still have one in your shop?" Me, "I have two!" He smiled like a proud parent. Then a car went speeding down the street and he said, "We need signs out here saying, 'This is not a drag racing track'." I said, "You sound like our other neighbor who used to say we should stand on the street with signs telling people to slow down. I used to tell her she could have at it but I'm not a 'Boomer' yelling on the side of the street—I'm an 'X-er', and we're all about xing-out a problem, like maybe nail them with a fire hose." He laughed and said, "I wouldn't want to get on your bad side." And just like that he went from being proud of my two extinguishers to contemplating why I really bought the second one.

Not to brag or anything however, I turned my Dad into a damn good code-writer during my shop years. I can't call it a skill, because I'd have no idea how to do it on purpose, but wow, do I ever have a talent for finding weaknesses and glitches in computer programs. (That's what I'm choosing to call it, rather than an oddity in how I approach things.) My Dad made me a "practice" database for the one I would be using after I switched over the store. He really didn't think it was necessary until I reminded him of what happened the first month I was open at the bookstore with that much more straightforward database and–voila!–he decided it might be a good plan after all. I used the practice program for my month-end bookwork, intending to transfer it all over to the "real" books when I was done; however, I crashed the program. When I tried to explain how it happened my Dad's eyebrows winged up so fast he could have flown away with them. My Dad, "What were you doing?" Then, "Never mind, I don't want to know. I'll just make it so you can't do it again." A few days later a very satisfied Dad told me, "I just figured out how to block entries so that no one can put in data that would crash the program. You don't really have to worry about that for ninety-nine percent of the people but that one percent." Me, "You're welcome. If you'll have a better end product, my job here is done." At the end of the month, and only a few tiny glitches later, I triumphantly waved a completed spreadsheet at my Dad and said, "Oh look, Dad! I didn't screw up anything in the computer program this month!" My Dad (dryly), "Let's see the final print-outs before saying anything rash." Then we were talking to friends and my Dad was explaining the program and he said, "If a user can create an error in a program, it's always the programmer's fault." Then he looked at me and said, "Unless it's Roxanne using the program. No one could anticipate the many ways she can create computer errors." Me, "I'm here to help!"

I'm pretty sure I had a clean record of sales people hanging up on me at the shop but really, how can you not see it as a challenge to make them do so? I got a call from someone guaranteeing me that forty thousand Cortezians would see the ad he wanted me to buy. I just laughed. He asked what was so funny so I asked, "Have you ever been to Cortez?" Sales guy, "I haven't yet had the pleasure." Me, "Then I'd suggest you go look us up on Wikipedia" and laughed harder. He asked, "Are you ever going to stop laughing?" Me, "Nope." And, he hung up on me.

Here's hoping he pursued the relevant info, learned there are less than ten thousand Cortezians, and laughed at himself.

Back to school in any town makes downtown donation alley for students trying to raise money for their various endeavors, which is what led me to thinking about what I'd include if I were to write a guide for young people soliciting funds from businesses for their school programs. (Otherwise known as what the ones who came into my shop were stuck listening to.): We would really appreciate it if the first time we met you was not when you showed up asking for money. Shopping at chain stores or on the internet but then coming downtown to solicit small businesses is not a sustainable model for us. So, maybe take a day to browse around the shops you are going to be hitting up for cash so that you can tell folks about what's available downtown and give us the impression that you are interested in the businesses that will be supporting your endeavors. Community means you support us and we support you. (They tended to look a little sheepish, but did look around.) It's great that your parents are accompanying you but if you want cash from me, you will speak for yourself and be able to answer questions about how the money will be used. If you are not interested enough in your program to understand the details, why should I be interested enough to help pay for it? Give us options for how we can support your program. We work off budgets, with lots of different people wanting a piece of it, and it's less awkward for all of us if we aren't the ones who have to suggest a way that we can support you that doesn't break our bank. Be polite. We love our community and are happy to support your endeavors but we don't owe you anything. On the heels of that lecture to one kid, I had a parent, who had not accompanied them, come into the shop. Apparently, their kid complained to them about me being such a meanie and all. That parent thanked me for reminding their kid that walking door to door asking for money isn't "work." Nice.

I was just sitting there minding my own business one day at work when a roly-poly bug dove out of the ceiling air vent and onto my head. It was semi-tucked in, not fully extended when it hit, so maybe a 4.5. Pretty impressive bounce and roll at the end though, so another 4.5 for a total score of 9.0. Me jumping up and dancing around like I was cheering it on? Total score 10. (One of my days in a bugshell.)

Sitting with Purpose. One big change that occurred when I was on a seasonal break was that a bench had been installed in the recess of the building next door to my shop. Apparently, not so much a place to rest as it was a new challenge for Cortezians as it had a "No Loitering" sign right behind it. I don't know about y'all but my sitting on a bench rarely looks purposeful; it tends to look a bit idle, aimless and purposeless. You know, the very definition of loitering. Well, except when I'm seat-dancing, but I'm pretty sure that's not what they had in mind.

My first job at the shop whenever I returned from any kind of break was removing dust-covers; second was sweeping the dust out of the shop. (Desert, after all.) Some might shy away from sweeping on a really windy day but seriously, if you angle everything right so it doesn't blow back at you, you then don't have to sweep your outside walk... it just blows away. And I thought I'd never use high school geometry.

Admittedly, I am a sentimental soul but wow, it so touched me, after Happy died, when a little guy, maybe two years old, plopped himself down in front of my A-frame sign on the sidewalk and started petting the depiction of Happy. That ended up being a more common occurrence than I ever would have guessed, and a double pleasure for me because they were always so gentle and I always got to appreciate that someone was teaching them that. Then came the day when I had a small person go by who'd been by with his dad shortly after I reopened for the season and had asked a bunch of questions about Happy. I heard, "Mom! That's Happy!" (From the tone, I'm guessing Mom heard a lot about Happy.) Then I looked up and saw the tot pointing all excitedly at the sign. So sweet!

I'm a fast-speaking person (though not a fast talker, mind you) who has always struggled with trying not to finish drawling Southerners' sentences for them. I have also long understood that puppers imitate their people. What I did not previously realize is that when you put those two things together you'd get me, in my shop with a Southerner and his dog, wanting to finish the drawling dog's sentences. Bark it out already! It's easy: woof, ruff!

I heard from a good authority one day (and when you read this you will have to agree that he is both good, and an authority) that my changing room is totally unnecessary. And, as far as he was concerned, any shirt that isn't a medium. Yep, had an older gentleman in the shop (many years at this, makes him an authority) who was choosing a t-shirt as a gift for a friend. He didn't need any help figuring out the size because, "Everyone can wear a medium, and if they can't, I can." And there's the good.

Wait, what?! You want Kokopelli playing the flute, without the dog, because you aren't a dog person? Are you insane? Giving up a chance for Happy-ness... with a dog named Happy? Sacrilege, in my shop! Get out. Go! (Yet another example of my impressive sales technique since they laughed, and bought. I'm tellin' ya, I should write a sales manual.)

Nineteen years! Nineteen! In my nineteenth year someone came into the shop and said, "This place smells great, like... *me nodding, already anticipating the inevitable "popcorn"*... pine!" Talk about throwing me off! Me, "You must work with wood." Man, "Yes! How'd you guess?"

Yes indeed, I did name the cross people in my front window. (Not cross as in angry... cross as in t-shirts hanging on one. We built wooden crosses for the display.) They kept startling me with their presence when I'd catch them out of the side of my eyes and I couldn't even curse at them using their names; which might just be why they did it– because I hadn't named them–which I guess means both kinds of cross may have applied. I decided to go with Myron and Win (that will only make sense to Harlan Coben readers.) because one was taller and looked like a big dude in comparison to the other, smaller one, which had a v-neck on it so I had to put a bandana in to hide the wood, which rather looked like an ascot. Besides, Kokopelli and Happy could have used an agent, and everyone could use a psycho that's on their side.

When you're wrong, you're wrong, no bones about it. I got to listen to two kids, looking at my sidewalk sign (Kokopelli walking behind Happy while playing the flute), and speculating, "Why is Kokopelli chasing down that dog?" Their ideas ranged from, "Maybe the dog took something," to "Maybe he got out of the yard," to, "Maybe he's running away because Kokopelli sucks at flute playing." When they wound down I piped up and suggested that maybe Kokopelli was following the dog, not chasing the dog. They said, "Ohhhhh" then, "Nah."

That generational moment when: you're talking about a drawing with a train in it for your tourist shop and you're feeling all steampunk and archaically historic by calling it an iron horse and your Dad pipes in with, "I rode one of the last steam locomotives runs on the northern route from the PNW to Chicago." And you realize that, dang, he's way cooler than you.

My friends and family all know I'm a terrible salesperson so they'd tell me things to tell potential buyers. I had the basics down, like I certainly knew the mugs I carried at my shop were pleasing to look at (because really, who wouldn't like looking at Happy?) and knew that they were user-friendly (good grip, and they kept liquids warmer longer) and that they were practical (microwave, oven and dishwasher safe) but what I didn't know is that they were also life-altering. I had a friend come in extolling the virtues of my mugs and she told me a new one: that the bottom is flat, so they don't accumulate water in the dishwasher. May sound like a small thing to some but for those who save energy by not running the dry cycle that meant that a dishwasher could be emptied top rack first, with no danger of dumping water on the bottom rack dishes. Straight-up-life-changing! You will never look at the top rack of a dishwasher the same way again! (She was so serious when she pointed out the flat bottom that I had to tease her a bit.)

"Sidewalk Mom" scores! A neighbor and I were outside talking in front of my shop when a bunch of bikers came back to their motorcycles. I told the one guy, "I've been guarding your water. You should not leave your water like that. Someone might put something in it." Other biker says, "You must be the Sidewalk Mom." We then gave them info on distance to Mesa Verde, etc., and water guy asked if there were any souvenir shops in that area, so I stepped aside and pointed at mine. Another guy says, "That's your shop? We really should go in, she was kind enough to watch your water, after all." I said, "The water guarding was free, no obligation but what is here can be found nowhere else." They bought, and I gave other guy a patch for his leathers–my version of a gold star.

I had a couple in my shop and when the lady saw my matchbox covers she exclaimed, "I will never buy another one of those again! I have beautiful ones from Germany that I've had for many years and they're just useless now. Once the striker pad is worn down there's no way to strike a match." Me, "But it's a matchbox in there, you just remove the whole box and replace it." Lady, " Yes, but, the striker pad won't work anymore after you do that too many times." We went back and forth a few times on that (her husband, "That's not an ink stamp? I thought that was an ink stamp," so he wasn't really part of the conversation), then I pulled the entire matchbox out of the cover to show her. She laughed so hard! "All these years, I never realized! I've just been putting new matches in, taping sandpaper to the sides. I'm so glad I came in here." Then she said she couldn't wait to get home to check hers, see if it was just that simple all along. If not, I suggested they could always try the stamp thing.

Quote of the day: A small person was looking at my totes and then she turned to her Mom and asked, "Mommy, can I be that dog?" Awwww!

Hey, if trying to manipulate me and putting your parents in an awkward situation got me a sale, I was good with that. Child (that I didn't know really well but did know), "Roxanne, you're so nice." Me, "Why, thank you." Child, "Do you own everything in here?" Me, "Technically, yes, but it's all for sale." Child, "Roxanne, will you give me that ornament for Christmas?" Horrified parents, "You can't ask her that!" Me, "I'll pass the request on to Santa, how's that?"

My downtown neighbors, Once Upon a Sandwich, hosted a Christmas tree for many years with tags for gifts to be purchased for kids in foster care. That tree was such a gift to all of us, as well. Downtowners would wait until customers picked all the tags they were going to and then we'd come together to fulfill the wishes for any who remained. For younger kids we'd hang out in toy aisles and ask parents if we could ask their kids for advice and those kids would get so excited to help. For older kids, we'd snag a theatre kid to take shopping because we wanted to make sure we bought rockin' stuff. Half my age and twice my shopping savvy, the young ones were such a help. My favorite was telling one of the young men that I was making him into my expert on all things young and cool and he responded, "I AM an expert on all things young and cool." No argument here. The spree we went on together was one of the easiest shopping days I'd ever spent. That was a really good tree. Brought joy to many.

Tourist in my shop, "You know, I just came here to smoke a doob and chill but I've now been to Mesa Verde, over Wolf Creek Pass, and the true kicker, over Red Mountain Pass. I am entirely done with Colorado!" (All twisty mountain roads. There are apparently some things that even legal weed just can't make up for if you're a flatlander. I would have people in my shop who'd been sent over Red Mountain Pass in their big RVs by Triple A and later their GPS who were still shaking from the experience a few hours later. We're not called the highest state for nothin', and that was before legal weed. Amazing views, though.)

When the cop shop was next to me, they hosted EMTs on occasion so that people could stop in for blood-pressure checks and the like. They had a blood bus out there one day, doing a blood drive, and I thought I'd help them out so I posted a sign I wrote for them on my shop door that said, "They take blood of all personality types: positive, negative, high-pressure, low-pressure, surface-mined or hidden veins. If you've got some to spare, they've got the place to share." Stood them a few pints, oh yes I did.

Customer, "I love this dog!" Me, "The pupper's name is Happy." Customer, "Until I walk out the door. Then the pupper's name is Sadie." Me, "Well, the customer is always right–once you've bought the right. Always refreshing to deal with someone who gets that."

Me, "I hope you're enjoying yourself in our area." Man, "I'm from France." Me, "Does that mean you can't enjoy yourself or that you are, by virtue of being French, always enjoying yourself?" (He fortunately spoke English well enough to get a kick out of that.)

Customer, "I'd spend good money to pass some time in your head but I'll settle for the hat." Me, "Since the hat isn't tin foil, I'm taking that as a compliment."

Oh yeah, I totally believed it was a legit Amazon call from a l'il ole Cortez, Colorado, return phone number telling me I needed to press one to update my account info lest I not receive my order. Why wouldn't I, since I'd had someone who occupies an alternate universe in my shop once telling me all about how Amazon is hidden in our hills; kinda like NORAD. I'm pretty sure that someone is now spouting their theories online but I can't be positive since they were anonymous.

I walked back and forth to work for twenty-three years and honestly, I just never knew what I might run into. I was walking home one day and such had been my day, I wasn't really surprised when I crossed paths with a construction worker who was hootin', hollerin', and wolf-whistlin'. Seriously, I had to tell the guy if he didn't stop, I'd have to call his mother, and while I was at it, maybe his mother-in-law, and tell them what a great husband he is. Yep, crossed paths with that construction worker husband o' mine, and what's totally offensive from a stranger was totally perfect from him.

My spreadsheet for the shop hated me so much that it seemed no matter what I did, it came up with an error, so Marty took over that part of the book work for me. So there's me, eating breakfast–the fabulous chocolate chip mint ice cream that Marty made the day before– watching him re-do the book work for the shop. Marty, "What's wrong with this picture?" Me, "Absolutely nothin'!"

Yes, Virginia (and every other state), there is a Penny Leprechaun–and it's people like me. I had a penny bowl at the shop and I would commonly say, "I'll take the pennies out of the penny bowl, make the change even." Some folks would try to hand me the pennies from the bowl and I'd say, "Thanks, but you can leave them in there." Invariably, they would look a bit confused and say, "But then you don't have them." Me, "I do have them, they are still sitting in my shop." For some reason, that cracked people up, and made them want to add other change to the penny bowl and feed my little pot of copper with other metals; which was all golden to me.

One undeniably good thing that came out of legalized recreational weed in Colorado: funny interactions with stoned tourists, "Oh, man. I really like that! (pointing at my rock-climbing "get a toehold" tote), but I've never actually done that." Me, "Well, it's not a prize you get for having done it. You can just like it. And I'm sure you've gotten a toehold on something at some point. Heck, your toes are holding your flip-flops on right now." (Cackling laughter from tourist.) "True! Why didn't I think of that?!" Perfect silence from me.

It amused me no end that in the "normal" course of events I'd know the names of countless puppers and yet very few of their humans. But, it's the way of the retail world. It was perfectly acceptable for me to ask a person their pupper's name but since I couldn't ask the pupper for their person's name, and asking a person's name in a retail shop (unless you've been chatting) is just a bit awkward to most, I generally wouldn't know. Except, I was aware of that so I'd say, "Nice to have met you, Aspen (a pupper I met one day) and Aspen's person." Consistently, the person supplied their name, sometimes a handshake, so it was as they were leaving (not arriving) that I was saying, "And I'm Roxanne. A pleasure to meet you."

It was always an adventure, working with one of my small business vendors. Unfailingly, every time I placed an order, something went sideways and the end product was not quite what I had in mind. (Colors different than ordered or the design was not where expected or the like.) Just one of those deals where you so know that it's going to happen that over the years, Marty and I took to trying to predict what it would be that time, but never were right. I liked that vendor a lot. They always took responsibility for the errors and offered to fix any problems on their dime but we found that the errors had their own kind of charm, so we never asked for that. Nope, we just eagerly awaited what the next thing would be.

And so it goes when you're a small business owner. I had a man come into the shop asking for the business owner, then telling me he's not from a PAC, a lobby or a special-interest group but that he represents people from all over the country who are interested in government and the Constitution and he wanted my representative to hear my opinion about some issue and if I'd fill out his form he'd mail it in for me for free. Me, "So, you're a volunteer organization?" Man, "No." Me, "So, who's paying you?" Man, "People from all over the country who care about the Constitution." Me, "So, how about a list?" Man, "I don't have one." Me, "So, this is a survey and someone's paying you for the answers? Right? How much if I fill it out?" Man, "You obviously aren't interested in our Constitution and I'm wasting my time here." Me, "Well, had you asked if I wanted to fill out a survey so only you could get paid, you wouldn't have wasted my time, either." Ended up being correct in my guess that he wouldn't be coming back to do his Christmas shopping in my place.

I had a man come in one day who'd recently moved this way from Johnstown, Pennsylvania. I told him Marty's Pop was John from Johnstown and he said, "So am I! What's his last name? I probably knew him or his people." So I told him it was Punchak (it was after the bookstore years so the name was no longer on the sign) and he laughed. Then he said, "Sorry for laughing but I could have guessed, a Polish name in Johnstown." So I told him about how when Marty's brother George was young, Marty's Uncle told him that their last name wasn't really Punchak, it was Taylor. But their Grandfather changed it to Punchak in order to be able to get a job in the Polish coal mines. The man started laughing even harder, then pulled out his driver's license to show it to me, and his name? John Taylor. (Yep!) So I said, "You know it used to be Tailor, right? Because you had one in your history. Someone changed it to a 'y' later." He said, "Really?!" I said, "I have no idea, but that's what we told Marty's brother when he tried to convince us their last name used be Taylor."

That awkward (for the other person) moment when: someone comes into your shop trying to sell you a service, looks at a piece of your inventory and says, "I could do this better." And you say, "I'm sure you could but since I'm the one who did it, which means it was free, I'm sure you couldn't do it cheaper." Yeah, there's no coming back from that.

One of my neighbors on Main Street was trying to learn to be "less nice," so she asked me for some advice. I had to tell her that step one is don't feel guilty because you think it's not nice to ask me for advice on how to be less nice. (Because really, you could tell she did.) What had prompted the request was that she had overheard an interaction about popcorn sweeping earlier that day, and liked how I handled it. I saw a bunch of popcorn on the sidewalk in front of the two businesses on the other side of the theatre when I ran up to the restroom and so, when I walked past one of the theatre kids on my way back (he was standing outside, doing nothing), I pointed out that sweeping it up would be the neighborly thing to do. He said, "That's not on the sidewalk I have to sweep." I said, "But it's obviously from the theatre." He said, "But I didn't leave it there and I get off in fifteen minutes and I'm just too tired." Me, "How about I suggest to the manager when they get back that they be too tired to write your next paycheck?" (I could understand their frustration about people just leaving the popcorn on the ground as I certainly never experienced a world where, when I was a kid, I dumped popcorn all over the ground and my folks didn't make me go to the nearest business and ask to borrow a broom or, if I couldn't locate one, pick it up piece by piece, but still.) One of the things my neighbor wanted to know was why I swept a piece of sidewalk in front of a certain place, considering that we didn't exactly get along. (Neighboring businesses did our best to stay on top of the popcorn when the theatre was overwhelmed, and the theatre always did nice things for us.) She said she knew she'd do it just because she'd worry about what they thought of her if she swept the rest and not theirs, but why did I, since past interactions certainly proved that wasn't a worry of mine? Pretty simple to me, really. What either of us thought of the other had nothing to do with getting the popcorn off the sidewalk before it was all smooshed and folks were dragging it into wherever they went. So yeah, it could be defined as nice, but mostly I just saw it as a common courtesy, even though the other place never returned the favor.

Who knew the Bee Gees would be the source of a gift I got one day? The dance studio across the street treated everyone on the block to

outdoor music, and an elder couple (all tourist stereotypes covered: Bermuda shorts, knee socks, straw hats, summer dress) treated the block to an outdoor dance. When they hit the spot where they could hear the music, the man busted a few moves, then settled into a lovely dance with his wife. A most perfectly wonderful sight to see.

That witch I worked for wouldn't even give me a lunch hour. Made me eat at my desk when there were no customers, so yeah, it was totally her fault when I was distracted by looking at all the people in Star Trek costumes, waiting in line for the movie, and I mistook my open thermos of water for the re-purposed gelato container with apple slices in it and dunked my fingers into it, instead. She thought it was funny, so funny that a few days later she made me bobble the pop I was getting ready to take a slug out of and caused me to pour it down the front of my shirt, instead of into my mouth. I might have been able to just blow that off (literally, blow it dry) except that time, there was someone in the shop, who laughed and said, "Been drinkin' long?" But hey, I was a master salesperson by then and so I said, "Just demonstrating how absorbent the t-shirts are…"

Well, lookie, there! Me, who has no fashion sense, should have gone into fashion design! The t-shirts I put in the front window of the shop were our sizes so we could wear them after the season. They were set up on wooden crosses we'd built (though not nailed to them), so some parts were folded under, some parts were exposed–and the exposed areas got indirect sun fade. We got many compliments, when wearing one of those tees about how cool the fade looked. I coulda been rich, if only I had thought to crucify a bunch of t-shirts on crosses.

You know, if the plows are going to pile up snow in a configuration that looks like mountain peaks, why not take a well-framed photo showing you're at serious elevation in the 14er state? (Colorado has more than fifty peaks over 14,000 feet and the highest low spot in all fifty states so no matter where you are, you are at altitude.) I managed to convince a couple of winter tourists of that, and then later got to hear all about the fun they had making themselves look like peak-reaching ice climbers. I had even managed a flag for them to plant at the top, made out of two postcards glued to a stick. A "Get Lit" postcard, that they'd be sending to friends to prove just how high they got in Colorado.

It matters, what you name your pupper. I had a person come into the shop to drop off a flier that said, "Our dog jumped out of the back of our truck at City Market (followed by the date, dog description, phone number, etc.). Goes by the name of Trouble, but won't answer when you call him." (No! Say it isn't so! A dog named Trouble would never cause any trouble!) Then it was the mail carrier's not so little four-month-old. (One of those breeds that will grow to weigh more than the mail carrier.) He brought him in on his day off so I could meet him. On introduction, the puppy was the perfect little paw-shaking gentleman, looking to impress. But then when he was told it was time to leave? He dropped down on his back and writhed like he was in agony. His name? Montague. ("I'd rather die than leave you!")

You know you picked the right three when: they aren't the ones your husband would have picked. Wife, "Come over here and help me pick out the bags for the kids." Husband, "Looks like you got it under control, I'm fine right here." Wife, "I want your opinion. Please come over here and help me." (Husband walks over to wife, points out the three he liked best.) Wife, "No, that one doesn't have anything on it that shows the area, I don't like the colors on that one, and that one would be for you except these are for the kids." Wife then buys the three she was already holding and reveals her true purpose in calling him over–as a place for her to dump her purse while handling the transaction.

Customer (while looking at postcards), "I travel a lot for my work and my boyfriend's been telling me I don't send enough postcards. What's the big deal? We talk on the phone all the time." Me, "Ignore for the moment that I'm a retailer and therefore totally on his side; my husband and I, many years ago when he was in the Army and before we were married, spent two years overseas from each other. And yeah, you have much greater phone access than we did but you can't reread a telephone conversation when what you really want is a hug. Written material means your words can hug him whenever he wants." Customer (tearing up), "Damn! You got me! I love stories like that. What's this cost and where's the nearest mail box?" (And I know she sent it because I kept stamps in the shop just so people could send without having to worry about acquiring those and when I stepped out of the shop some minutes later, I saw her dropping it in the blue box down the street.)

You maybe shoulda done a little research before you road-tripped all the way from Maine to Colorado just so you could catch a legal buzz in peace (and ostensibly see the sights, but really, not), just in case you step into the cute little shop with the ancient character and the Happy pupper and run into your fellow PTA member—who also came from Maine to actually see the sights—so that you could actually talk about those sights instead of mumbling away because you don't know what they are. And yes, you absolutely should thank the nice shop lady for the timely save by making a purchase. (Who needs TV when you have Main Street?)

I was talking about our puppers with a tourist in the shop who rather condescendingly pointed out that her dogs were award-winning show dogs: cost a mint, transported from Europe, etc. Me, "Oh, we just got lucky with ours; got her free from in front of City Market. Total mutt–and she STILL won the best french-kisser in the county award. On to the state level next!" The way she curled her lip at me? Would have done any junkyard dog proud.

I had a Professor who used to say to me all the time, "You have to stop using me as your grammatical editor, Roxanne." To which I always replied, "Why? You're so good at it!" And, there's plenty of evidence out there that I still subscribe to that general philosophy: let those who are good at it do it, though I do get it right every now and again. I had a lady who came in and told me that she was an English major, and loved the idioms/puns in my shop, but found the name of my shop a little misleading, "Kokopelli's Getaways sounds like a travel place." Then she thought about it and exclaimed, "You're right!" (Even though I hadn't said anything.) "That is grammatically correct. You are depicting Kokopelli's Getaways, not planning other people's." Got it, second time!

My first-ever exchange amused me no end (a wrong- sized gift. It wouldn't have amused me at all if some no-taste person was returning something with Happy on it because they didn't like it), because the lady came in digging around in her purse for the receipt and then started fretting aloud when she couldn't find it. I said, "It's all good. You don't need the receipt. It couldn't have been bought for you anyplace else." She laughed and said, "Well duh, that's why my friend bought it for me: custom design." (Truly, it's such an amazing feeling when someone not only likes what you've created, but likes it enough to gift to another.)

I loved my brick-and-mortar shop and never really had any interest in taking it online, if for no other reason, because I just didn't want to deal with some of the ridiculousness that comes with that. Like, I once mailed a mug to someone who emailed me a while later and told me it had a crack in it but they weren't writing for a replacement or refund because they were pretty sure they broke it, they just wanted me to know in case I wanted to change something on my end. Uhm, still not exactly sure what it is I could have changed on my end to stop someone else from breaking something, but, okay.

I can't even begin to guess the amount of time I spent cleaning dog slobber off the full-length mirror at my shop (puppers sure do like seeing themselves in the mirror. "Let me kiss me!"), but it was enough to make me start thinkin' that would be a good place for a hidden camera. Then I could open a virtual kissing booth, charge folks to get dry pupper kisses. That's an online business I could have gotten down with. "Get your licks in!"

I had a shop open across the street from me wherein the owners were retired and new to retail. When I went over to introduce myself, they asked if I had any observations about small towns to offer. They had been closed a day the week before and it was obvious by people yanking on the door and then looking around that they hadn't put up a sign saying they were going to be, so my observation for them was that small-town folks get irritated when you are closed without a sign so unless it's an emergency, put one up. It can just say you will be closed, but people like ice-breakers so if you can, tell them something they can ask you about when they come in; and they will come in, just to ask you about it. They said, "I guess that explains your sign saying, 'Aussie friends visiting so I am playing hooky today'." Me, "Yes. And that sign I put up saying, 'Stuck at home waiting for a service technician. We all know what that's like. See you tomorrow. Roxanne'." And, of course, the all-time favorite sign in my shop window, "Kokopelli's Getaways is Closed Today. (It's the rain. I could melt, and then who'd look after the flying monkeys?!)" When you work for a witch...

What I confirmed every tourist season? As much as dogs would get incredibly happy just to be allowed in the shop, people would get incredibly happy to look behind a curtain. I needed a front cover for one of my cabinets at the shop where I kept extra stock but the way it was structured made using wood awkward so I thought to go with a fabric cover, but couldn't find a fabric print I liked, so Marty made me one. (He made a stamp that we used on plain fabric. And like the desk Marty made me, I had many inquiries from folks about how they could buy it.) Then I learned that if you tell someone they are welcome to lift it up and go through what's in there you don't have to say it twice. Folks weren't even disappointed when they didn't find the Wizard of Oz.

When Susie's Gifts on Main (formerly Susie's Hallmark) closed for retirement, I really missed them. They brought so much beauty downtown with their aesthetically pleasing window displays and their big smiles and warm greetings. But even more, Susan was Main Street's very own Great Pumpkin. We have a yearly Halloween Treat Parade (and all the surrounding activities) that is her legacy. I think we had maybe fifty kids the first few years but by the time I closed shop, we were at over six hundred. Such a good time was had by all, I always felt like a teenager again. (Or, who knows, maybe that was just the break-outs I'd suffer after getting into all the Halloween candy.) Many folks dressed up: Susan, who went all out each year, my Mom as a black-clad good witch. Even the twenty-somethings that worked on Main dressed up. So fun to see all the costumes, that is until the year a skateboarder decided to dress up as a "redneck" and then started describing how he acquired his clothes and we figured out that the jeans he bought from the thrift store to complete his outfit had been MINE! (Though I guess it beat them being used as granny jeans...) It became such a big event that I'd order copious amounts of candy in advance. Then it was me, exercising amazing restraint while sitting in my shop with hundreds of candy bars and not eating any of them. (Uh-oh... gotta go now... can't reach the keyboard... seems my nose is getting in the way.) Then it was waiting for all the little monsters to show up (settle down, it was a Halloween Treat Parade... I can call them that), and even some older kids. (I had nothing against older kids coming out to the treat parade but it did quite amuse me to hear parents talk about how you shouldn't judge older kids going out and trick-or-treating; let them be kids as long as possible. As if they weren't really thinking, "A few more years of taking candy from MY baby.") Then all the "too adorable for description" costumes coming our way. (That's how I'll always speak about them, anyway, since aside from the kids who announced what they were (loved that!) we didn't always know. I thought the little Incredible Hulk that Marty called a Ninja Turtle was actually going to turn into the Hulk and straighten out that misconception.) Then they'd reach my block and Marty would start carnival barking, "Eyeballs, eyeballs, come get some eyeballs!" and the kids would hold out their bags and, after we gave them theirs, pull one out and say, "I got eyeballs!!" Sooo cute! Such a fun day every year, and totally worth the sugar hangover zombie aspect downtown would have for a few days after. Many thanks to Susan and her staff.

"In" versus "at", because some folks would rather quibble with you about your merchandise saying, "in the Four Corners USA" than just say it's not what they were looking for. You can indeed be "in" the Four Corners, as we are a region. You cannot be "in" the Four Corners Monument as there's no "in" there, only an "at." Well, also an "on," yes, and an "under" and indeed you could get in a plane and get "over" it... like I was with that conversation, soooo over it... but, I digress. Really, I was a retailer, I understood that not everyone was going to be buying what I was selling. Now that we have that straight, please excuse me since reminding myself of that conversation causes me to need to go bang my head "against" a wall.

People laugh when I talk about that witch I used to work for but there are people writing articles about her. Yep, "Five Types of Annoying Colleagues" and she was all of them, in one! Took credit for everything I did. Check. Tried to one-up me whenever I had a good idea. Check. Amateur psychologist trying to get into my head. Check. Oversharer–like I needed to know everything she knew. Check. Advice columnist–

always trying to tell me what to do. Check. The downside in working for a sole proprietor, let me tell ya.

It's hard out there for small business owners. I needed to pay a deposit for work another small business was doing on a project for me so I called to give the owner my credit-card number. She jokingly promised to apply it to my order and not to use it to buy Christmas presents for her employees; not because she'd be above doing that, but because they were being all whiny and difficult so she wasn't feeling kindly disposed toward them. Me, "Yeah, that witch I work for never buys me anything." Owner, "I thought you own your own business?" Me, "Exactly! If I was being whiny and difficult, totally her fault! But did that matter to her? Noooo!" She so guffawed. When I received my order and called to say that all was in good order she passed along a thank you from her employees for her attitude adjustment. Seems Scrooge wasn't her customary spirit and they were glad to have her back.

Ah, Moms, you can always count on them to go above and beyond. At the height of the passing-out-hugs craze, I had a lady (a stranger) fling open the door of my shop and walk in saying, "I'm passing out hugs today and you know what I learned? People are so hug deprived, they don't know how to do it right!" Me, "Full disclosure in the interest of fair play, I'm married to a hugger and am pretty good at it." Lady, "Prove it!" *Hug the lady* Lady, "Okay, so you might just be better at this than me. And by the way, my son's band is playing at the Legion Saturday night, seven to eleven, five dollars a head." It reminded me of how, when I found a bunch of my business cards in my Mom's things after she died, I saw my folks' phone number written on the back of them. It took me a minute, and then I realized she'd have done that so when she gave people their new cell-phone number, she was giving them my business card at the same time. Free advertising. I so love getting those hugs from beyond time and space.

I may not have been on top of the Mount for this common lecture but at 6200 feet, definitely on high desert ground when delivering it. "Commandment: Thou shalt hydrate. Where thou goest, thou shalt bringest water. Thou will drink enough water to not feel thirst, as thirst is a sign of dehydration. Thou will drink it steadily and thus avoid headaches, nausea and other ailments. Thou will have fresh water for thyself and thy fur friends. If thou does not, friendly local businesses will provide it. If thou follows this commandment, thee will add significantly to thine's enjoyment of this piece of Lord's country. And don't forget thy sun-protecting hat. If thou dost not have a cap, thee will find a really cool one right here. Now, go forth and vacationify!"

Cell phones definitely changed up one thing for me, I no longer had kids ask to use my phone to call parents who forgot to come pick them up after the movie. (I used to get quite a few on Free Movie Tuesdays, most of them later in the summer, when parents thought the kids should just stay through all the showings, give them a break, who cares if it's the same movie?) So, I was a little surprised one day when I had a young lady come in to ask. And I had to admire the way she tried to capitalize on an opportunity when speaking to her Mom. She said (yes, if you were using my phone I was eavesdropping: the cord only went so far and it was a small shop), "This is why I need a cell phone, Mom!" I almost felt bad for her that I still had a landline there since by the way her face fell, the Mom evidently pointed out that she'd managed okay without one, but since the Mom decided to buy something when she picked up her kid, I couldn't quite work myself up to much sympathy.

When an icebreaker goes down like the Titanic: When my hair started really graying, a number of folks felt it appropriate to give me unsolicited advice on what I should do with it. So, I took to playing "Let's Make a Deal" and would say, in a freezing tone, "How about you don't comment on any of my personal choices, like that I don't dye my hair, and I won't comment on any number of yours that I could name." (I loved the look people got. "Who, me? What could you possibly have to say about me?!")

Most people came into my shop because they were Kokopelli fans and loved that we gave him a dog, or because they didn't know Kokopelli at all and wanted to hear about local lore. However, I did have a few come in that were attracted to my shop for reasons that hadn't previously occurred to me. I had people in my shop one day who stayed in town past the time they intended just so that they could bring their dog in. We don't know how Happy lost her tail, but she came without a full one. So too was their pupper without a full tail, but they knew that was due to an accident. It was still healing and their young grandchild was concerned that the dog wouldn't be able to do everything he used to. Enter Happy, doing all those things we had her doing in the drawings: without a tail. Going home with stickers of every drawing as presents for the child to show her that tailless puppers can still do things? Too sweet!

Archaeologist approved! Being the archaeological capital of the U.S. (your agreement with that statement is not required for us to maintain it), it was not a surprise that I'd get archaeologists in my shop every now and again. Like with everyone else (because I didn't know they were an archaeologist just by looking at them), I asked them if they were familiar with Kokopelli. And, of course, they were. However, I had one tell me he was interested in hearing how I describe Kokopelli so I said, "One of the most common figures on the rock art from the Anasazi/Ancient Puebloan Period." Archaeologist, "That's okay, then."

I laughed, while thinking, "Your approval of that statement is not required for me to maintain it."

Falling asleep while trying to get some paperwork done late one night and then waking yourself up because your mouth has fallen open and your cheek is flappin' with every exhale, just like a pupper's, is, I'm thinkin', the only way I could have gotten away with sleepin' on the job since even that witch I worked for laughed about that.

At some point, I realized that I was the second-longest individual resident on my downtown block. The only one who had been there longer than I had was my upstairs neighbor, Sam. He is a very nice man. Always had a friendly greeting and he could be counted on to help the other businesses in the building with anything from shoveling snow, to fixing projectors, to not complaining about the loud music coming from downstairs. And, he forgave me when a reporter came by, asking questions for a news story, and I totally threw him under the bus by sending the reporter his way. There's an old saw that says that in small towns, your business neighbors won't even talk to you until you've been there about five years and at about the five-year mark for me I jokingly said to him, "Well, it's about time for you to start acknowledging me, except you've been talking to me all along. I bet that's because after one conversation with me, you knew it was going to be your fate to atone for all your sins by having R Lord as a long-term neighbor." He said, "Why, yes! And I learned I wasn't nearly as sinful as I thought." Awww! Yes, that's just how nice he is.

The oddest thing I learned about selling t-shirts? Some people don't like the word "unisex," which my t-shirt sizes were. At one point I thought we might just find ourselves building more shelves and setting up separate men's and women's sections... carrying the same shirts... so as not to confuse anybody, but was saved from that because I had both crew and v-necks, which evidently makes all the difference. (Why? Your guess is as good as mine.) The oddest thing about my t-shirts to customers? I priced all my adult t-shirts the same even though there were two styles and the sizes ranged from extra-small to 3x. No, they didn't all cost the same when I purchased them, and yes, I took a hit on potential profit. So, why do it that way? Because some things just stick with you and I had a friend say to me, long ago, that she wished that just once she could go into a store and not feel like she was being punished for being shapely. That's why.

I always enjoyed the tourists, wherever they were from, but I did most especially enjoy when Japanese tourists came in shopping for Christmas gifts because though everything I sold in my shop was made in America, Marty was not, he was made on a Naval base in Japan (his Pop was career Marine Corps), and delivered there on Christmas Day. I always knew how it would make him smile when I told him one of our designs was headed there, and I loved how it made the tourists smile when I'd say, "Yes, everything in my shop is made in America; however, the best Christmas gift I ever received was made in Japan."

Yes, Marty was in my display window to fix things on occasion. And yes, he is organic. But he was NOT made in America, so he thought I should just stop singing, "How much is that Marty in the window?"

I love when you get to tell people about the positive impact they have made on others. A friend of mine worked as a manager in a retail environment. She had retired from that position but young people she trained still worked there. I had a couple of them come by to tell me how disturbed they were by how current management approached the cash till. They'd been told that as long as their till was over, it was all good; their only concern was underages. However, when my friend trained them, she taught them that a balanced till is best but under is better than over because over means that you are stealing (even if inadvertently) from your customers. Current management rolled their eyes when the young people told them that, as they didn't share my friend's view. The young people knew I was still in touch with their former boss and wanted me to tell her thank you for teaching them better. It was a pure pleasure for me when I got to tell her how the values she taught were moving forward with the people she trained.

Double shifts, the death of my hopes and aspirations. I was telling a theatre employee one morning that now that they were open all day again it's a good thing that their daily shifts rotate so I wouldn't look to any individual quite like the glutton I am for Reese's and chocolate-covered almonds and he said, "Oh, I'll be here all day, but it's not like you come by two or three times a day, anyway." Well, darn it, no going back that day...

In my twenty-three years renting from the theatre I saw a lot of people come and go through there: Eight managers, I think, and many employees. One of the managers, Diana, was a rather quiet lady, who took the job to supplement her retirement income and because she enjoyed people. A dignified person, who I never heard swear, even when she had major cause. A funny person, in a very understated way. She started what would become a kind of tradition wherein she'd point me out to new employees and tell them what kind of chocolate I'd want if I came in, and we'd both get a smile when they'd reach for it before I could say because the employee would always be so excited that they were in the know. (Which, now that I think about it, makes all the chocolate I ate her fault! No matter why I went over there, someone pulled out a candy bar, and I then had to buy it. Wouldn't want to hurt anyone's feelings, right?) She was such an integral part of what made it just plain fun to be there, not the least of which because of the times she got a little agitated by the marquee sign. Fiesta Twin has an old-school, really cool marquee; one which requires people to physically change the reader board. That led to, "Things you never expected to hear from a former school teacher" like, "Oh drat, I have to spell it right because I don't have enough t's to spell it wrong." (The movie airing? "STRAIGHT OUTTA [or maybe in a pinch, OUT OF] COMPTON.") Because the marquee is such a fancy one, it's a popular photo op for tourists so it wasn't uncommon to see people stop to take pictures. However, it was uncommon to see many, many of them over the course of one day. So many that I finally went out and looked and what did I see?

"BAD MOMS

SAUSAGE PARTY"

So rote was it, for folks to just put up the titles, that not in a million years would it have occurred to her how that could be read. And boy was she red once she was made aware. (I had to tease her and ask, "Weren't you paying attention when I said one of the ways I pick new authors is to line up their titles and see what story that tells?") She took it all in stride (though did flip the titles, much to the dismay of those who missed the photo op) and had a little fun with later titles. My favorite was one that she posted just for me:

"FATE OF THE FURIOUS

SMURFS

GOING IN STYLE"

My thanks to Diana, for all the good times.

I never would have guessed that asking people if they know who Kokopelli is would lead to so much skin baring (even though he is known, among other things, as a fertility God.) but yeah, there were times when I would ask someone if they knew who Kokopelli is and they'd answer by removing items of their clothing to show me their Kokopelli tattoo. (Thankfully, all inked in socially acceptable places.) But what no one had? Kokopelli with a dog. For showing me dogs, when theirs wasn't with them, folks had phones, and they'd pull them out to show me their dogs and then explain to me why even though Happy wasn't just like them (they being of different breeds), she was like them. It's the spirit, not the body, that drew them. If only humans could get there, right?

Turn that Frown Upside Down!
I've read a number of articles talking about what people from other countries find strange about Americans, and our big smiles commonly make the lists. For example,
"When a stranger on the street smiles at you:
a. you assume he is drunk
b. he is insane
c. he's an American"
(From a Finnish Reddit user.)
I even had tourists ask me about all the smiling we do. "Are you all just high or what?" I would explain that there are studies out there that argue that the greater the immigrant base of a country, the more folks are likely to smile at each other–the non-verbal way of communicating a desire to socially bond with people you may not share language or cultural histories with. And that the smiles are big because we value happiness. (Or at least the pursuit of it…) Which was pretty much an eye roll to most, and then they'd start looking at my inventory and say, "Oh my God! Even the dog is smiling!" Me, "And, her name is Happy." Big smile

I know that when the school district cut the school week down to four days that it was a major disruption to both kids and parents but did they ever ONCE consider the inconvenience to folks like myself, who relied on the recess bell at the elementary school next to our house to tell me it was time to go to work? Spend all that time proving Pavlov out and then, after many years, I had to look at the clock–and then give myself a treat for remembering to.

If you ever receive a social-media friend request from me, DO NOT ACCEPT! It would be that witch I used to work for. She'd so totally clone me, if she could. If you let her on your page she'd do to you what she's been doing to me: troll you, poke at you, start arguments just for the sake of it. She'd post good pictures of food (without telling you I made whatever it is) and bad photos of her friends. She'd use stickers and gifs and memes propagandists could only dream of trying to match. She'd friend all your friends like an airborne virus, then chain mail you links that will hang on you like a bad suit of armor. Just sayin'.

I regularly dealt with people in my tourist shop who weren't fluent in English and I wanted to try to learn at least a basic phrase in multiple languages in order to greet them, so I put one through an internet translator. Then I just kept changing the "translate to" language for a number of languages and, inadvertently did an internet translator version of the game "telephone." (For those unfamiliar with the game: you pass a whispered phrase on from one person to the next, the goal being to see how the phrase changes along the way and how it is finally heard by the last person.) I typed in, "Good morning. If I can help at all, please let me know." (Something I actually said that morning at the shop.) I put it through ten languages and what I got back at the end was, "Good Morning. I can not help you, please." (Which was sometimes true, but still.) Back to the old standard it was: when all else fails when trying to explain Kokopelli to someone who didn't speak much English, default to the universal language of slang, "A cool dude with an awesome mutt." Worked every time.

I was feeling lucky the morning I chanced to be looking out the window when the dance instructor across the street was lost in her own groove. A rare treat, to see someone who moves so well dancing solely for themselves, just for the joy of it. Thinkin' she probably wasn't feeling as lucky if she was looking out her window later that day and caught me dancing around trying to work out the pins and needles I got from sitting on my foot too long (think: Joe Cocker), but it did bring a smile to a person coming in to shop.

All sorts of people talk about how much they hate(d) taking tests; fear of failure and all that. Can't say it's ever been a favorite activity of mine either, but for different reasons. For instance, I had to fill out some paperwork for the credit-card company that took a bit because I couldn't decide if the line saying, "Title of Business Owner" was a trick, therefore I should fill it in "Business Owner"; a desire to know what I do, thereby I should fill it in, "President, CEO, CFO, COO, Admin Asst, Secretary, Clerk, Mail deliverer, Intern, Tech, Janitor, Customer Service Rep, HR, Supervisor, Street Sweeper, Sign Maker, etc."; or a request for a copy of my business license, proving I hold title to the business. Ach, too much to think about and I didn't want to slight any of my selves so I just left it blank. Where's multiple choice when you need it?

The irony. I was yakking with one of the theatre kids and they told me Thanksgiving had been all about people in line talking self-righteously about how big corporate stores should not open and people should not shop on Thanksgiving so that workers can be home with their families– while they were preparing to hand over their cash to, no, not a robot– to get into the movies. It never seemed to occur to them that maybe the turkeys the theatre employees wanted to spend the day with were not the ones going to the movies.

Living the retailer life: Lady, "I LOVE these! But, Kokopelli should be paddling in this one." Me, "But, it's a motorboat." Lady, "But he should be paddling. You should change it." Never mind that she'd be back in Minnesota by the time that happened, I got right on it, oh yes I did not.

Not everything was all hearts and flowers on Main Street, there were also some arguments that went on: parking, sidewalk cleaning, who has the rights to a particular body. Yep, downtown went all "Tales from the Crypt" one week when a disagreement broke out over an individual's remains. In what I can only describe as a truly macabre twist, a fellow downtowner apparently brought their own body bag to the funeral home where the deceased was residing in order to retrieve the body so that they could be the ones to bury him. Seems their plan was to put the corpse in their car and drive away with him. How nuts is that? And how is one meant to interact with someone that you now know is driving around with a body bag at hand, ready to go?!

When everyday use of the internet was still new, had you asked me at two o'clock one day I'd have said that the most absurd part of my day was a neighbor calling ME to help with a computer problem. (I'm not known for being on the cutting edge of technology; however, I did end up taking care of the problem; not by solving it, by working around it, something I am known for.) But nope, that wasn't it. By three o'clock, it was the, ahem, locking myself out of my own computer when I got back to my shop.

Well now, there's a compliment. I definitely had people come into my tourist shop who'd say, "I don't get it." (Which was amusing to me on the face of it to me because– hello–"get" idioms.) And we often called the stuff in my shop silly because of what we had Happy doing and her big grin, but I had someone come in one day looking for something "corny" and they said my stuff was too nice to be called corny. So there ya go; they did smile when they saw the stuff, but not corny.

All hail the internet. It has so many useful purposes, like a page devoted to biker slang, which is just the thing when someone has been sitting right outside your shop revving an engine for way too many days in a row, so loudly that you couldn't converse with customers in your shop. Yep, the web made it so I could curse them out in language they'd understand, "Why is it I'm being baffled by a blown bike?! Better secure that brain bucket and armor you ape-hanging, four-banging, lawmaker cuz I'm dropping the hammer down and once I'm done throttling you I'm unleashing my yard shark to school you in the real meaning of thrashing it and rippin' it up! I'll put the binders on her when you pick up some manners to go with that donor cycle. Damn SQUID!" (Made me feel better, anyway–and they liked it so much they asked for the paper I was reading it from and then parked elsewhere.)

We all laugh at the ridiculous label warnings on everyday objects, but then one day you look out your window and think that you've finally noticed a parade before the marching band kicked in, but no, it was just a bunch of folks gathering to watch the guy across the street removing his business sign by hanging onto a stepladder tied to a rope that they had thrown over their second-story roof and you think, "Yep, there's the guy who thought his cape could make him fly."

I had a guy in the shop one day who had recently moved to the area for his wife's job and just could not say enough about how much he hated the place. He had an endless list of bad experiences he wanted to talk about. I finally interrupted him to say, "My husband really enjoys this line he heard on the TV show Justified. It goes, 'You know, if you meet an asshole in the morning, you met an asshole. If you meet assholes all day, maybe you're the asshole.'" Stopped him in his tracks and then he looked at me like he was trying to decide whether or not to add me to the list of bad experiences... and then he laughed! Told me I was probably right since he does seem to attract those situations. He'd come in with a really nice dog, one who spoke on command, so I suggested that in future, he let the dog speak for him.

It's definitely a nice reminder that you live in a good town when firewood flies off the back of someone's truck and you see folks go after it like candy thrown from a parade float, and all they are thinking about is helping the driver prevent an accident, and not how useful it would be with the cold temperatures.

And, more tales from the alternate universe: After I closed my shop, Marty went to a mailing place to send off some inventory I was donating and then balked at the rates and decided to take it elsewhere. The counter person stopped him and told him if the items were from a business, he could get a cheaper rate. Wait, what? Yes, I'd heard of cheaper rates for the recipient being a business address (and ours was a non-profit, so them too), but why exactly would the return address matter when you brought it into the shipping place? Not much, evidently, since Marty misremembered my old business address and the one he gave them wasn't actually my address at all. Had I known about that, I could have been selling my neighbors' addresses for cheaper shipping rates for years!

I was so happy when I was finally done dealing with the credit-card processing company, I can't even. A while before I closed, the small company I signed on with was absorbed by a large one that caused me one headache after another, most particularly with the large company illegitimately charging me for things they had no right to charge me for. (Note to self on the subject was: Credit-card companies are in the position of strength [POS] at the point of sale [POS] which is why the person of suspicion [POS] doesn't need the power of suggestion [POS] to understand how often they are a POS [piece of shit.]) It came down to threats on my part for them to finally refund the last of the money they owed me but, what else can you do? "Either you refund it, or I use up significantly more than eighty dollars of your time dealing with me. Your choice." I had to appreciate the lady who actually did all the work to get it done. She said, "You're the funniest pissed-off person I've ever dealt with and I'm enjoying talking with you, so that might not go the way you are thinking."

When the shop was a bookstore, people assumed I had a house full of books. I don't. I love books and I read, a lot, but I am not a collector, so I do not have a lot of books. Once it was a touristy shop, folks assumed I love Kokopelli and had a lot of him at home. I don't. The truth is, he was the secondary figure for us, that we co-opted as the Queen of Happy-ness's regent because he is so popular. We had to pass that job on after she died so we passed it on to him. And we love him for taking it on.

When I closed my shop, I had many accounts to close that were associated with it. For one of them, you couldn't actually log in and do that, you had to talk to a person at a central clearing house; and that person wanted me to answer my security questions, which started with, "Your favorite movie?" I don't have one, and totally couldn't remember what I put, so I started randomly naming movies, but he stopped me at two and told me if I went for three I would invalidate the whole process. I offered to try for the other question but he said he'd have to find a different way to verify I was who I said I was since both had to be answered correctly, but he did tell me that the question was my favorite food and I then knew I wouldn't know that answer either because mine is so obvious (a chorus of "ice cream!" was just shouted by those who know me), which meant I would have used something based on my mood at the time. (Like how my shop passwords for things I was annoyed by having to do, like file endless forms, were always abbreviated expletives.) I had been rifling through my paperwork while talking to him and I finally found where I had written the answers down (yes, I wrote them down. Feel free to slap my wrist; however, the worst a hacker could have done to that account was pay a bill for me, with no stored info to do it with) and what was my mood? Carrot, which I'm sure represented to me, at the time, that I'd like to forgo that and hit the website with a stick. When I relayed them to the customer service guy he laughed, "Yeah, that's the first time I've ever seen carrot and I thought it odd. Now it makes perfect sense."

You're not crazy if someone is just screwing with your mind! After spending an hour online unsuccessfully trying to figure out how to close a retail tax account and then calling and having to listen to the endless FYI message about all the things I could (and should) do online, and then multiple menus and long wait time, someone came on the phone and told me, "You can't do that online." Seriously?! And you couldn't put something online telling me that? I then went to print the form that the agency rep told me I couldn't file online and the first paragraph of the instruction page said, "If you have a login you can close your account online at____." (You couldn't not have a login since you paid those taxes online.) However, since all my attempts to do it online had previously failed, I mailed off the form. But I didn't see an account closure in a reasonable period of time, so I called again and, oh joy, I was told how I should have done it online. Revenue employee, "There just must have been a misunderstanding." Me, "My fault, I'm sure. I did once understand, 'No, you can't do that' to mean, 'Go for it!' but since I'm not a teenager and you're not my parents, I assumed he meant what he said. My bad." At some point, interest and fines for being sane in an insane world just start looking inevitable.

I was really ready to be done with all the shop-closure-related things by the time the end neared, so I made a general announcement: "Let the countdown begin! Four more days until I tell that witch I work for to take this job and shove it! Been practicing in the mirror." But I also knew I was going to miss it, so it was followed by," Wait, what? That witch I work for is firing me? After all I've done for her? Man!"

The day I opened my shop I was given a master key to the theatre because my upstairs neighbor, me, and the theatre functioned as a little community that looked out for each other and took care of things for each other. About ten years in I had a man come into my shop and ask to use that key to access the theatre so I asked, "Who are you?" and he said, "The owner." Me, "Well then, yes, you may borrow my key." It was such a pleasure, to exist in a world where that could happen.

It's always a little sad when reality intrudes and people have to stop unreservedly believing in the magical: Santa Claus, the Easter Bunny, the Tooth Fairy. And so surely the person most saddened when I decided to retire from retail was Marty, when he realized that the royal purse (otherwise known as his wallet) would no longer be mysteriously re-stocked by Queen Happy and Kokopelli. (Cash from an ATM just not nearly the same.) For my part, I thought some practices are just meant to continue. When I opened the bookstore the theatre manager at the time gave me a counterfeit-detecting pen, and I spent much of a day marking money, just for the heck of it. It was something I hadn't thought of when I opened the shop, but good to have. It just so happened that I had a new neighbor move in right before I was moving out, so I brought her a pen, with all hopes that all the money that crossed her palm was real. (Except maybe like one three-dollar bill, just so she could see the ink change.) Then I passed the lucky money bean a friend had made me when I opened the bookstore and my penny dish that was a gift from another friend onto another business. While I was doing that, I ran into one of the "kids" (by then in his thirties) who used to work at the theatre and he said, "Every time I go by your old shop and see it emptying out, it makes me a little sad. New theatre employees won't get to have the 'Roxanne experience.'" I laughed and asked, "And was that a good thing?" He said, "Oh yes. I always knew if

I needed anything or wanted to talk about something you were right next door." (Patting my heart.)

Shopkeeping wouldn't really appear the logical choice for someone who dislikes both shopping and selling and yet, for so many reasons and in so many ways, it was exactly the right choice for me. I'm known to say that I don't collect anything, but Marty corrected me once by saying, "But you do: you collect moments, and people's stories." And oh, the people I got to meet and know: My chats with all the folks at the sandwich shop on my way through in the morning, and the most wonderful brownie the owner gave me on a day when I was being all cranky. Not quite the Wild Turkey she wished she'd had (in her best Jack Nicholson voice), but it still killed the bug up my butt; my fellow retailer and her employees, who created the most welcoming environment in their shop and always had a smile and a wave. And what's not to love about an employee from her shop, who heard our much-loved visitors had returned home, and so brought me punch and cookies because she knew I'd be a little sad and wanted to give me a pick-me-up? My upstairs neighbor, always on the move but never so fast he didn't stop for a greeting; my theatre neighbor being thrilled that the latest movie was "Pan" so she didn't have to worry about whether or not she had enough letters for the reader board, propping my sidewalk sign against my door when I forgot to put it away, all the employees reaching for my favorite candy when I'd go in with cash in hand; having a little chat with the owner of the Four Corners Free Press when she was on her rounds, refilling the newspaper racks; my newest neighbor coming by just because she wanted to share her excitement about something great that had happened for her; the delivery drivers and the mail carrier stopping for a few extra minutes to chat and jam with my tunes; a dog rushing over with his tail wagging hello; chatting with the artisans who turned our vision into works of art; having a human emoji come into my shop who was so effusive that she made me want to buy my own stuff; saying, "Accent! Where are you visiting us from?" and enjoying a few minutes speaking with many different people from many different places; the strangers in cars you waved at because they yielded the right of way when you were walking back and forth to work so that you could cross. There are a lot of good reasons to shop local. High on my list would be because every time you do you are entering a neighborhood and all that suggests: good people, with a real appreciation for community, doing their best to live the American Dream.

Afterward

Some time after I closed my shop(s) I decided to do some word challenges related to the shop drawings. Every piece of writing had to have Happy's name in it, idioms related to the idiom on the drawing (I had to get creative with a few of those since there weren't any), language that was specific to the activity, a message, and plays on words that amused me. (Like calling this "afterward" instead of afterword, since this is about what came later.) Nothing about what I came up with was pure: not the verse/prose/poetry, not the trickster or fable elements, not anything. Were you expecting different when writing about a mutt? I wrote them for myself, but later decided to make them into a book to close the circle from bookstore to Happy shop to Happy in a book. And thus, "Kokopelli's Getaways with Happy" is a book that includes all the drawings from the shop, with verses for each. It is both an acknowledgment of all the people I met in my shop years who understand the value of a good book and a steadfast friend, and a way for me to honor the many times someone said to me, "I just really like this happy dog," to which I'd say, "That's actually a capital H, because that was her name, Happy."

144

Other books by Roxanne:

The Truth and Nothing but the Truth . . . According to Ruth

Kokopelli's Getaways with Happy
Authored as Lord Punchak
Written by Roxanne and illustrated by Marty

If You're Happy and You Know It, Wag Your Tale

www.ingramcontent.com/pod-product-compliance
Lightning Source LLC
Chambersburg PA
CBHW050519100526
44581CB00001B/41